Dear Samir,

Wish you a very

Happy B'Day!

From Rajeev & Amit

100 GREATEST QUARTERBACKS

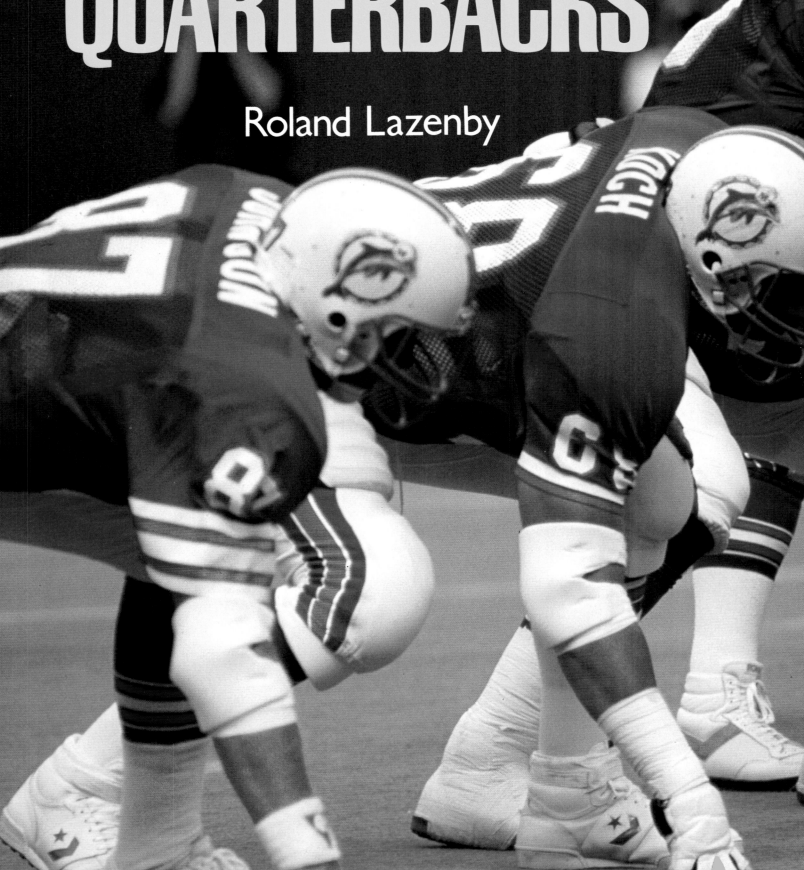

100 GREATEST QUARTERBACKS

Roland Lazenby

Crescent Books
A Division of Crown Publishers, Inc.

INTRODUCTION

Sonny Jurgensen once remarked that playing pro quarterback 'is like holding group therapy for 50,000 people a week.' The position is among the most visible, the most demanding in all of sport. And as Jurgensen or any Hall of Famer will tell you, no other role draws more emotional response. Within the course of the game, quarterbacks and their fans cover the gamut of love and hate, admiration and spite. There is seldom a middle ground.

'Pro football gave me a good sense of perspective to enter politics,' Congressman Jack Kemp once said. 'I'd already been booed, cheered, cut, sold, traded and hung in effigy.'

With the passions of the audience in mind, I ventured cautiously into the task of selecting 100 great pro quarterbacks. It proved to be an elusive pursuit because playing quarterback involves a tricky mix of talents. Leadership rates high. But so do passing, competitive spirit, physical toughness, presence of mind, mobility, excellent vision, the ability to read defenses rapidly, luck, determination, and a knack for winning. Add to that a high level of self confidence that occasionally borders on arrogance and you have a reasonably amorphous recipe.

The real help in evaluating quarterbacks comes from Paul Brown, who once remarked that to judge a great signal caller you have to look at where he winds up. With that in mind, I put particular emphasis in my evaluation on the winning of championships. Those who took their teams to the top were viewed more favorably. Next I relied on statistics and records, with some thought for awards and Pro Bowl appearances.

I also liked the toughness factor. Playing pro quarterback is a brutal vocation, frequented by the regular threat of broken noses, dislocated shoulders, fractured hands and torn ligaments. Anyone who questions that should watch a replay of Lawrence Taylor sacking Joe Theismann on Monday Night Football in November 1985. Theismann's career ended with the sickly snap of his shin.

Even more crippling is the gradual battering quarterbacks take over the weeks of the season. It takes substantial courage, the kind often evidenced by Dan Fouts, to stand in the pocket play after play, week after week, season after season, waiting until the last possible instant to make the throw, just before the weight of the defensive rush comes crashing down.

Football is a base game of blocking and tackling by large, powerful men. The quarterbacks carve artistry out of this crude landscape, making a deft pass here, executing an efficient handoff there, always calming and directing and orchestrating the action around them. Without a good quarterback, a team quickly descends into chaos.

In essence, the challenge of quarterbacking is using a mix of wits and athleticism to neutralize a violent opponent. It is one of the great challenges in all of sport. At one time or another, the players included on the following pages have met that challenge at the highest level of the game. Some are Hall of Famers, players for the ages. Others are mere journeymen, whose careers are memorable because of their longevity or because they included a particularly productive season.

The publisher has asked me to close the book by ranking the top 100, a presumptuous, subjective task for any sportswriter. There are about 40 truly great quarterbacks. The next 60 or so are a toss up. For help in evaluating the group, I sought the opinions of Paul Zimmerman of *Sports Illustrated* and Steve Hartman of the Los Angeles Raiders. I am deeply indebted to them for their input.

Copyright © 1988 Bison Books Corp.

The 1988 edition published by
Crescent Books, distributed by
Crown Publishers Inc.
225 Park Avenue South
New York, NY 10003

Produced by
Bison Books Corp.
15 Sherwood Place
Greenwich, CT 06830, USA

Printed in Hong Kong

Library of Congress Cataloging-in-Publication Data
Lazenby, Roland.
    100 greatest quarterbacks.
    1. Football players—United States—Biography.
2. Quarterback (Football) I. Title. II. Title:
One hundred greatest quarterbacks.
GV939.A1L39 1988   796.332'092'2 [B]   87-34332

ISBN 0-517-65840-2

h g f e d c b

Page 1: *St Louis Cardinals quarterback Jim Hart looks for a receiver in a 1973 game against the Washington Redskins.*
Previous pages: *Dan Marino and the Miami Dolphins meet the New York Jets, 1986.*
Opposite: *Jim McMahon of the Chicago Bears looks downfield as he eludes a San Francisco 49er defensive rush.*

Ken Anderson

Ken Anderson was a third-round draft pick out of little Augustana College for the Cincinnati Bengals in 1971. He remained a vital part of the team for the next 15 years, and in the process became a fixture near the top of the NFL's quarterback ratings.

In that time, he compiled some whopping statistics, completing 2654 of 4475 passes attempted for a .593 career completion percentage. He amassed 32,838 yards with 197 touchdown passes against 160 interceptions. He passed for more than 300 yards in 19 games and captured the league passing title four times – 1974, 1975, 1981 and 1982. He was also selected to play in the Pro Bowl five times (1974, 1976, 1977, 1981 and 1982). He led the league for three seasons in having the lowest percentage of passes intercepted.

His career highlights include completing 30 of 46 passes for 447 yards and two touchdowns to beat Buffalo in a Monday night game in 1975. But his grand moment came with the 1981 season when he led the Bengals to the AFC championship, with a 27-7 victory over the San Diego Chargers. In that superb performance, Anderson completed 14 of 22 passes for 161 yards and two touchdowns.

In Super Bowl XVI the Bengals fell 20 points behind Joe Montana and the San Francisco 49ers. But Anderson rallied his team, completing 25 of 34 passes for 300 yards and two touchdowns. With a little more time, he might have caught the Niners, but the rally fell short at 26-21 when the clock ran out.

Anderson was the league's MVP and consensus All-Pro for 1981, when he passed for 3754 yards and 29 touchdowns against only 10 interceptions. For the season he completed 300 of 479 attempts. Anderson holds several NFL passing records, including highest completion percentage in a game, 90.91, by connecting on 20 of 22 passes against Pittsburgh's strong defense on 10 November 1974; most consecutive passes completed, 20, against Houston in the Astrodome on 2 January 1983; and highest completion percentage in a season, 70.55 for 1982, when he connected on 218 of 309 passes to break the legendary Sammy Baugh's record of 70.33 set in 1945.

Steve Bartkowski

A first-round draft choice out of the University of California in 1975, Steve Bartkowski ran the offense of the Atlanta Falcons for a decade. In that time, he set club career records for passing yards (23,468) and touchdowns (154). He threw for 31 touchdowns in 1980 while leading the Falcons to the NFC Western Division crown with a 12-4 record. For that effort, he was named to the 1981 Pro Bowl.

Although he passed for 3830 yards in 1981 (a club record), he did not take the league passing crown until 1983 when he threw for 3167 yards and 22 touchdowns against only five interceptions. Bartkowski's percentage of interceptions, 1.16, was the second lowest in league history.

His 1984 production was rated the third most accurate in league history when he completed 181 of 269 attempts for 67.29 percent. Only Ken Anderson and Sammy Baugh have rated higher.

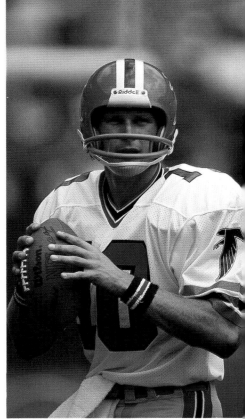

Opposite left: *Veteran Ken Anderson calls his signals for the Cincinnati Bengals.*
Opposite right: *Anderson fades back for a pass. He carried the Bengals to the AFC Championship and Super Bowl XVI in 1981, where he completed 25 passes for 300 yards and two touchdowns.*
Above: *Steve Bartkowski, a permanent fixture in the Atlanta Falcon offense for ten years.*
Left: *Bartkowski rifles a long one. 'Bart' set numerous club records for Atlanta and earned a 1981 Pro Bowl nomination as well as the 1983 passing crown.*

Sammy Baugh

Samuel 'Slingin' Sammy' Baugh of Texas Christian University was the second player selected in the 1937 draft, signed for the then outrageous sum of nearly $20,000 per season by Washington Redskins owner George Preston Marshall. He would go on to play 16 seasons of superb pro ball, and would pass for an astounding total of more than 22,000 yards, a little better than 13 miles.

In his first pro game, Baugh completed 11 of 16 passes. He would finish the season with 1127 yards, becoming only the second passer in NFL history (Green Bay's Arnie Herber was the first in 1936) to pass the 1000 yard mark in one season. This stellar performance took the Redskins all the way to the title game versus the formidable Chicago Bears. Like Red Grange before him, Baugh showed the league its future that day, hurling an all-star passing performance into the face of the wind at bitterly cold Wrigley Field and sending the favored Bears to defeat, 28-21. Despite the weather, he turned in numbers typical of the pro game of the 1980s – 17 of 34 passes completed for 352 yards and three touchdowns.

Driving his team to the NFL championship in his rookie year was a grand beginning for what proved to be a legendary career for Sammy Baugh. For six seasons – 1937, 1940, 1943, 1945, 1947 and 1949 – he was the NFL's top-rated passer. For seven seasons he led the league in percentage of passes completed. In 1945, he turned in the second most accurate season in the history of pro football, completing 128 of 182 attempts for a whopping 70.33 percent, a mark bettered only by Cincinnati's Ken Anderson in 1982. In 1947, Baugh shattered all previous passing yardage records by completing 210 of 354 attempts for an amazing total of 2938 yards.

Lest modern quarterbacks take his skills too lightly, it should be noted that Baugh also played defense full time for the Redskins. In 1943, he led the NFL in interceptions with 11. He also led the league in punting from 1940 to 1944, averaging 51 yards per kick in 1940 and better than 45 yards per kick in the other seasons.

His wide range of skills helped carry the Redskins to the title game several times, but not always to the title. Baugh's Redskins were on the unfortunate end of the NFL's all-time great upset, the 73-0 victory by the Chicago Bears in the 1940 title game. In the 1942 title game, Baugh threw a 39-yard scoring pass to carry Washington over Chicago, 14-6, registering something of a redemption from the 1940 embarrassment. The two teams again met in the 1943 title game, and although Baugh passed for two touchdowns, the Bears won 41-21.

His 1945 season still stands as the second highest rated passing performance, 109.9, in league history.

Only Cleveland's Milt Plum has had a better season, 110.4, in 1960.

Baugh retired from competition in 1952 and was elected to the Hall of Fame in 1963.

Above: *Hall of Famer 'Slingin' Sammy' Baugh of the Washington Redskins shows his passing form. The legendary Baugh, who was also a threat as a punter and defensive back, threw for over 22,000 yards in his career.*

Pete Beathard

In college, Pete Beathard treated the football world to one of its greatest Rose Bowls, when he led the top-ranked Southern Cal Trojans past second-ranked Wisconsin, 42-37, in 1963. Beathard completed eight of 12 passes, four of which went for touchdowns in taking the Trojans to the national title.

He was then taken in the first round of the 1964 draft by the Kansas City Chiefs and the Detroit Lions but wound up as the 'air' apparent to George Blanda with the Houston Oilers.

Beathard directed the Oilers to the 1967 AFL Eastern Division crown with a 9-4-1 record. But in the championship game, the Oilers got greased by the Oakland Raiders, 40-7.

Against the Kansas City Chiefs in September 1968, Beathard completed 23 of 48 passes for 413 yards and two touchdowns.

Top: *Sammy Baugh, shown here on the sidelines, was one of the most honored and respected players of his time.*

Right: *Houston Oiler Pete Beathard rolls out and looks to pass in a 1967 game against the New York Jets.*

George Blanda

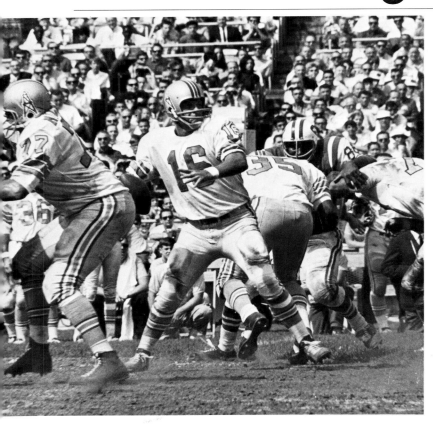

Above: *Houston Oilers quarterback George Blanda sets up in a well-formed pocket and prepares to fire a pass.*

Right: *This 36-yard field goal by Blanda with two seconds remaining gave the Oakland Raiders a 37-34 victory in a 1975 game.*

George Blanda earned a name as the old man of pro football, with a playing career that spanned 26 years, from 1949 to 1975. As a passer and placekicker, he got what one might call the 'complete football experience.' He went from being a journeyman signal caller for George Halas and the Chicago Bears to the role of hired gun for the Houston Oilers, and then for the Oakland Raiders.

After 11 largely uneventful seasons (Blanda led the NFL in completions in 1953), the Bears released him in 1959, at age 31, just in time for the birth of the AFL. He became a star quarterback and kicker for the Houston Oilers, leading his team to three championship games and throwing the winning touchdown pass in the AFL's first championship game. Next season he set a pro record by throwing 36 touchdown passes, and was the AFL's leading passer that season with 3330 yards. With that AFL fame, however, came the ignominy the next year of setting an all-time record for interceptions in a season, 42 in 1962. Yet his passing effort for the Oilers was prodigious. He led the league from 1963 to 1965 in the number of passes attempted, and against Buffalo in November 1964 he put the ball up a whopping 64 times.

In 1968, Oakland Raiders Coach John Rauch picked Blanda up as a kicker and backup quarterback, and he soon became a miracle worker. When first-string quarterback Daryle Lamonica was injured early in game six against the Pittsburgh Steelers, the 43-year-old Blanda came in and threw three touchdown passes for a 31-14 Raider win.

Blanda came in as quarterback again in the fourth quarter of the game against Cleveland. He drove his team to a tying touchdown, then worked them into field goal range minutes later with only three seconds left. From the Cleveland 45, he kicked a 52-yarder for a 23-20 win.

The following week, down 19-17 to the Denver Broncos with four minutes left, the Raider coaches decided to insert Blanda for a last drive. He took the team 80 yards and won the game with a 20-yard TD pass to Fred Biletnikoff. The cap on the streak came the next week against San Diego, where with seven seconds left, Blanda beat the Chargers, 20-17, with a 16-yard field goal. The Raiders won the divisional championship on the momentum of his magic.

At the end of the season he was voted the AFC's Most Valuable Player. He retired from the Raiders in 1975 at age 48. Six years later he was inducted into the Hall of Fame.

Terry Bradshaw

Terry Bradshaw earned his share of individual honors over the course of his career, but his identity as a professional began and ended with his role as the throwing arm in the Pittsburgh Steelers dynasty of the 1970s. Bradshaw of Louisiana Tech was selected in the first round of the 1970 draft by Steelers coach Chuck Noll. Other wise draft choices would lead the Steelers to four Super Bowls between 1974 and 1980, with a defense including Mean Joe Greene, Jack Lambert, L C Greenwood, Jack Ham and Mel Blount, and an offense starring running backs Rocky Bleier and Franco Harris. By 1971, Noll had his young team in playoff competition. That December, Bradshaw acquired the first chunk of his reputation as part of a legendary pass play.

With a score of 7-6 and 22 seconds left in the AFC playoff game versus the Oakland Raiders, the Steelers faced a fourth and 10 at their own 40. Bradshaw blazed the ball over the middle to running back John 'Frenchy' Fuqua, who was covered by Oakland safety Jack Tatum. The ball, Fuqua and Tatum came together at the 35. The two players fell, but the ball ricocheted toward Pittsburgh running back Franco Harris, who nabbed the ball at his ankles and raced to the end zone to win the game. Myron Copeland, the Steelers' radio announcer, dubbed the incredible play the 'Immaculate Reception.'

Although the Steelers' season ended the next week at the hands of the Miami Dolphins, Pittsburgh would make the playoffs again the next season, only to lose to Oakland. Finally in 1974, a vital ingredient was added with receivers Lynn Swann and John Stallworth. They were mere rookies when the Steelers used their defensive viciousness to subdue the Minnesota Vikings, 16-6, in Super Bowl IX. Bradshaw completed nine of 14 passes for 96 yards and a touchdown.

In 1975, for the second year in a row, the Steelers took the AFC title from the Oakland Raiders as Bradshaw completed 15 of 25 passes for 215 yards. He also threw three interceptions. In Super Bowl X, backed up by the infamous Steel Curtain defense, Bradshaw completed nine of 19 attempts for 209 yards and two touchdowns for a 21-17 win.

The Steelers faltered in the 1976 and 1977 playoffs but found their form again in 1978. They stormed past Denver, then Houston in the AFC championship to meet their old rivals, the Dallas Cowboys, in Super Bowl XIII. Bradshaw put in a superb performance with 318 yards and four touchdown passes and took home the game's MVP trophy as the Steelers won, 35-31. The victory made them the first team in NFL history to win three Super Bowls.

Bradshaw and the Steelers continued to ride high in 1979. In the AFC title game, Bradshaw completed 18

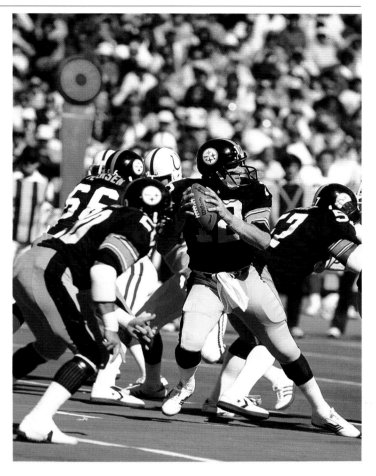

Above: *Pittsburgh Steeler Terry Bradshaw in action against the Colts. Bradshaw quaterbacked the Steelers to four Super Bowl victories.*
Left: *Bradshaw threw for over 300 yards two times in the Super Bowl.*

of 30 for 219 yards and two touchdowns. The Los Angeles Rams, led by quarterback Vince Ferragamo, provided surprisingly stiff opposition in Super Bowl XIV. They maintained a lead through the third quarter, until Pittsburgh zoomed away with the game, 31-19, on two fourth-quarter scores. Though he threw three interceptions, Bradshaw completed 14 of 21 passes for 309 yards and two touchdowns. With this performance, he had set Super Bowl records for career touchdown passes and passing yardage.

By 1980 the Steelers' luck had run out. But during the glory days of the 1970s, Terry Bradshaw had taken the Steelers to four Super Bowls, and come away with four trophies.

Zeke Bratkowski

Zeke Bratkowski came out of the University of Georgia in 1954 to write his name in the record books as a rookie with the Chicago Bears. Then he drifted into the life of a backup, first with Chicago, then with the Green Bay Packers. But unlike most backup quarterbacks in the NFL, Bratkowski had his championship moments.

Fresh out of college in 1954, Bratkowski passed for 1087 yards in 130 attempts for an average gain of 8.36 yards, the second highest average for a rookie in the history of the league. For the next five seasons, Bratkowski played backup for the Bears, then joined Vince Lombardi and the Green Bay Packers. He played a major role in the Packers' drive to the 1965 NFL championship. Bratkowski had filled in for Bart Starr and pushed the Packers to several key victories on their way to a 10-3-1 season. They wound up in a tie with the Baltimore Colts for the Eastern Division title, and met Baltimore for a playoff game to decide who would go to the NFL championship.

Starr was injured on the first play of the game, and Bratkowski filled in like the old pro that he was, completing 22 of 39 passes for 248 yards in Green Bay's 13-10 overtime win. The Packers, of course, went on to whip the Cleveland Browns for the 1965 title. Bratkowski also did duty behind Starr in Super Bowls I and II, which adds to his credentials as the 'master backup.'

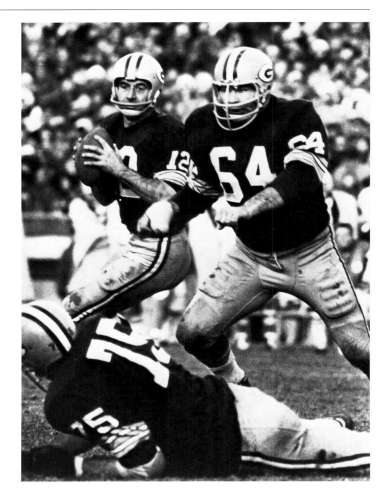

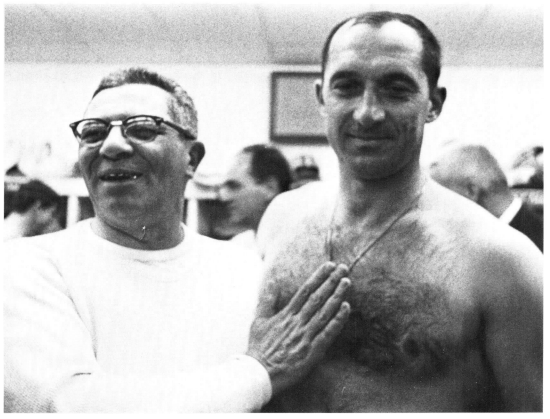

Above: *Zeke Bratkowski of the Green Bay Packers sets up behind reliable protection from All-Pro guard Jerry Kramer (64).*
Left: *Packers coach Vince Lombardi with reserve quarterback Bratkowski, who replaced the injured Bart Starr in the 13-10 sudden death playoff victory over Baltimore on 26 December 1965.*
Opposite top: *San Francisco 49ers quarterback John Brodie led the NFL in passing in 1970 with 24 touchdowns and 2941 yards.*

John Brodie

Some quarterbacks have had the good fortune to play with teams with vicious defenses and league-leading running backs. Others have had to struggle, carrying their teams on the strength of their arms and the endurance of their wits. For much of his 17-year career, John Brodie fell into the latter category. And as fate would have it, when his team was finally powerful enough to rise to the NFC championship in 1970 and 1971, Brodie would be visited with a plague of interceptions. Both years, the Dallas Cowboys stood in the 49ers' path to the Super Bowl. And both years Dallas advanced.

Regardless, Brodie's career statistics and accomplishments speak for themselves. He completed 2469 of 4491 attempts, ranking him sixth on the NFL's all-time list of completions. He ranks ninth on the all-time list in touchdown passes with 214. He holds the same all-time ranking for yards gained passing with 31,548. For three seasons – 1965, 1968 and 1970 – he led the league in both completions and total yardage. In 1970, he was the NFL's highest rated passer with 2941 yards and 24 touchdowns.

On the strength of Brodie's performance, San Francisco had the NFL's most potent offense in 1970. On the other hand, the 49er defense gave up 267 points. Still, the team won the NFC's Western Division with a 10-3-1 record and eliminated Minnesota, a strong

defensive team, in the playoffs. In the NFC championship against the Cowboys, Brodie and the Niners battled to a 3-3 tie at the half. He would complete 19 of 40 passes in the game for 262 yards, but the Dallas defense would press him into two key second-half interceptions, leading to a 17-10 Cowboy victory.

The San Francisco defense tightened for 1971, giving up a respectable 216 points as the 49ers again won the Western Division, with a 9-5 record. In the playoffs, Brodie quarterbacked the Niners past Washington, 24-20, then witnessed a replay of his struggles against Dallas in the NFC championship game as the Cowboys won, 14-3.

Finally, Brodie seemed to have the Cowboy riddle solved in 1972, as he led the Niners to a third straight Western Division title with an 8-5-1 record, including a 31-10 win over Dallas. The Cowboys, however, came to the playoffs as a wild card team. Brodie again seemed to have their number, pushing his team to a 28-13 lead late in the third period. Then Roger Staubach, who had been injured most of the season, came off the bench and mesmerized the 49er defense. When the San Francisco receiving team failed to cover an onsides kick late in the game, Staubach directed the Cowboys to a 30-28 comeback. Brodie could only watch from the bench, his hopes dashed a third straight year. He retired after the 1973 season.

Ed Brown

The team of the 1940s, the Chicago Bears, fell into the gloom of an also-ran in the 1950s, finishing at the middle or back of the pack each year in the NFL's Western Conference. Then in 1956, aging coach George Halas retired and Paddy Driscoll took over the team. Ed Brown, the Bears quarterback, found his pace and led the league in passing with 1667 yards and 11 touchdowns. Buoyed by his performance, Brown directed the offense to a league-leading 363 points during the 1956 season as the Bears finished 9-2-1 and won the Western crown.

The storybook might have gone a chapter further, but the Bears fell behind early in the NFL championship game to the New York Giants and Charlie Conerly. Brown struggled to lead his team back but the passing game presented the Giants with two interceptions. They cashed them and their numerous offensive opportunities in for a 47-7 destruction of Brown and the Bears.

The lopsided outcome had taken the joy from Brown's fine season. In recognition of his ability, Brown was named to the Pro Bowl in 1956 and 1957. In 1959, Brown had his best season, passing for 1881 yards. Over an eight-year career with the Bears he threw for 9698 yards.

Rudy Bukich

Rudy Bukich carried the Chicago Bears to respectability in 1965 with a passing performance that topped the NFL. For the season, he completed 176 of 312 passes for 2641 yards. He tossed 20 touchdown passes and only nine interceptions to claim the league passing crown. He directed the Bears offense to 409 points (the second highest total in the league) and a 9-5 record, the fourth-best in the NFL.

A Southern Cal quarterback, Bukich joined the Bears in 1958 and played nine years, throwing for 6254 yards and 46 touchdowns. Although owner/coach George Halas expected a great deal from Bukich, he never became a consistent quarterback capable of taking the Bears to further championships. The Bears won the 1963 NFL Championship under Bill Wade, but failed to dominate again until the 1980s.

Below: *Ed Brown of the Chicago Bears hands off to fullback Rick Casares in the 1956 playoff game against the New York Giants.*

Opposite top: *Rudy Bukich, who played for the Bears from 1958 to 1967, steps over from the one-yard line for a touchdown against St Louis.*
Opposite bottom: *Paul Christman made a winner out of the Chicago Cardinals in the late 1940s.*

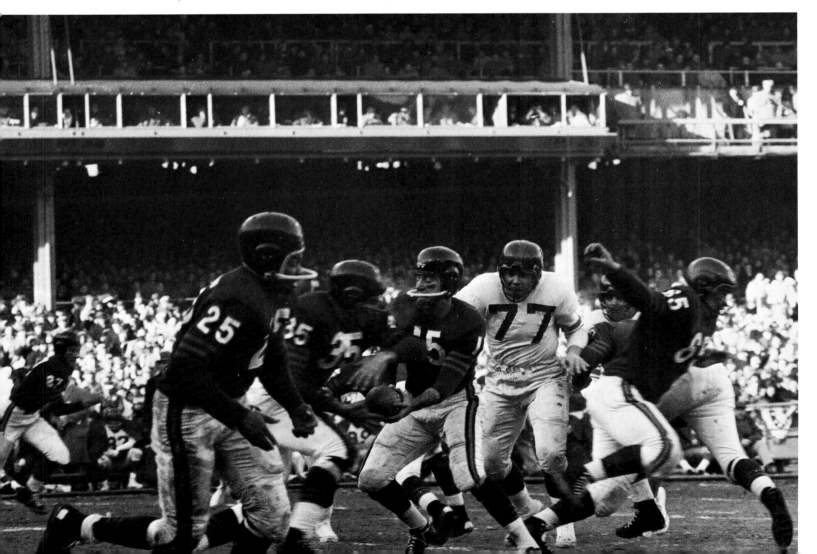

Paul Christman

Paul Christman, a star at the University of Missouri, came to the Chicago Cardinals in 1945 and helped them rise to the top of the NFL in two short years. During his rookie season, the Cardinals sat at the bottom of the NFL's Western Division with a miserable 1-9 record. Two years later they claimed the crown with a 9-3 record and an offense that racked up 306 points in 12 games. That season, Christman became only the third quarterback ever to throw for more than 2000 yards in a year. He completed 138 of 301 attempts for 2191 yards. Christman broke Cecil Isbell's record from 1942, but Washington Redskins great Sammy Baugh passed for more than 2900 yards in 1947, bettering Christman's performance.

In the 1947 title game versus the Philadelphia Eagles, Christman passed for only 54 yards, but directed the ground game masterfully as the Cardinals won, 28-21. Halfbacks Elmer Angsman (with two 70-yard touchdown runs) and Charley Trippi (with a 75-yard punt return) ran wild. The crowd of 30,000 at Chicago's Comiskey Park had plenty to cheer about.

Chicago again mastered the Western Division in 1948, this time with an 11-1 record, as Christman passed for 742 yards. For the regular season, Christman directed the offense to an incredible 395 points. The Cards met the Eagles once again for the championship, and as deep snow fell, Philadelphia edged Chicago, 7-0.

Christman, however, had mastered the pro game. In a few short years, he had taken a loser to the top.

15

Dutch Clark

A muscular 180-pounder, Earl 'Dutch' Clark graduated from little Colorado College and joined the Portsmouth Spartans for the 1931 season. He helped the team to a second-place finish in the league standings for 1931, 1932 and 1933. Then in 1934, G A 'Dick' Richards bought the Portsmouth Spartans, moved them to Detroit and renamed them the Lions.

Teamed with Clark in the backfield were fullback Leroy Gutowsky and halfbacks Ernie Caddel and Frank Christiansen. In 1934, their defense ran seven straight shutouts as they went 10-3, losing twice to the Bears and again finishing in second place. The tables turned in 1935 as Clark and the Lions went to the championship with a 7-3-2 record. Few people believed they had a chance. But in the title game at the University of Detroit Stadium, played amid sleet and wind, they whipped the Giants, 26-7, with a power ground game.

Also a top-notch kicker in his day, Clark led the NFL in scoring for three seasons – 1932, 1935 and 1936. For

Dutch Clark with the 1938 Pontiac presented to him by the Lions.

each of the eight seasons Clark played in the NFL, his team had a winning record. He retired from football after the 1938 season and was inducted into the Hall of Fame in 1963.

Charlie Conerly

Charlie Conerly played 14 seasons as quarterback for the New York Giants, from 1948 to 1961, and in the process gave the franchise some of its best years.

He had a whopper of a rookie season in 1948, setting a record for first-year quarterbacks with 22 touchdown passes.. His rating as a passer, 84.0, is the third highest for a rookie in the history of the league. For three seasons – 1950, 1956 and 1959 – he led the NFL in the lowest percentage of passes intercepted. In 1959, he was rated the league's top passer with 1706 yards gained and 14 touchdown passes against only four interceptions. He holds Giants team career records for yards (19,488) and touchdown passes (173).

His real reward came with the 1956 season, when he guided the Giants to the Eastern Conference title with an 8-3-1 record, then supervised a 47-7 blowout of the Chicago Bears for the NFL championship. The Giants claimed the title in Yankee Stadium where, despite icy conditions, Conerly pushed the New York air game to 222 yards on 11 of 20 passes.

Perhaps his most memorable moment came in a losing effort, the 1958 NFL championship, labelled by many, including NFL Commissioner Bert Bell, as 'the greatest game ever played.' Conerly drove the Giants to a 17-14 lead in the fourth quarter only to see the Baltimore Colts tie the game and then win in sudden-death overtime.

Conerly and the Giants won their division again in

1959 with a 10-2 record, but saw the Colts claim the championship a second time, 31-16. In 1976, Conerly's 1959 season as a passer was given a 102.5 rating, then the seventh highest in league history.

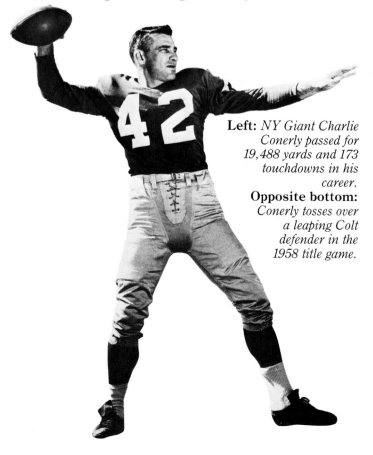

Left: *NY Giant Charlie Conerly passed for 19,488 yards and 173 touchdowns in his career.*
Opposite bottom: *Conerly tosses over a leaping Colt defender in the 1958 title game.*

Jimmy Conzelman

Jimmy Conzelman's résumé ran the gamut of football in its formative years. With George Halas he played on the Great Lakes Naval Training Station Team of 1918 that won the 1919 Rose Bowl. A 6-foot, 180-pound quarterback, he joined the NFL with Halas, playing the 1920 season with the Decatur Staleys (forerunners of the Chicago Bears), then played for two seasons each with the Rock Island (Illinois) Independents and the Milwaukee Badgers. Conzelman moved to Detroit in 1925 and founded the Panthers there. For the 1927 season he sold his interests in the team and moved to the Providence Steamrollers as a player/coach.

There, in 1928, Conzelman realized his dream, building the Steamrollers to the NFL championship with an 8-1-2 record. His playing career ended in 1929, but Conzelman continued coaching.

In 1947, he again was champion, coaching the Chicago Cardinals to the NFL title with a 28-21 victory over the Philadelphia Eagles in the title game. He was inducted into the Hall of Fame in 1964.

Jimmy Conzelman: quarterback, coach, Hall of Famer.

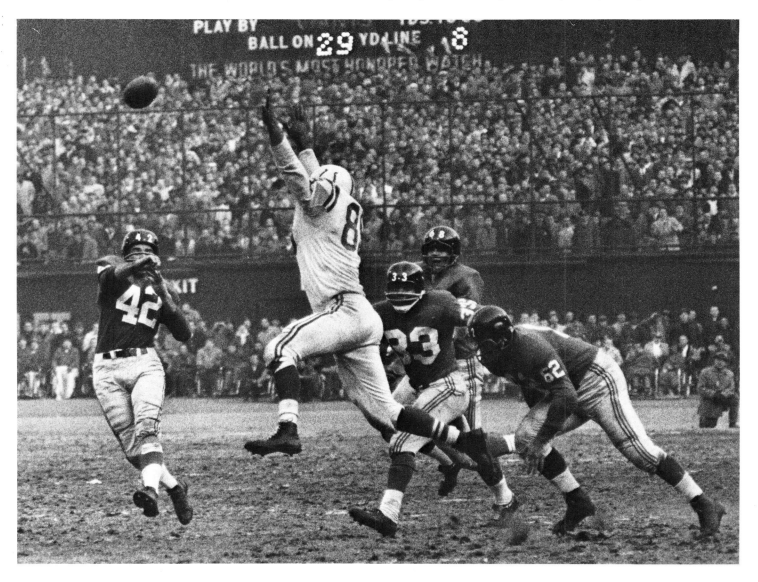

Greg Cook

Greg Cook showed enough promise in his rookie year to convince veteran observers he had the potential to be one of pro football's greatest quarterbacks. But then, after one dynamic season, injuries snuffed out his career.

A first-round draft pick for the Cincinnati Bengals out of the University of Cincinnati in 1969, he completed 106 of 197 attempts for 1854 yards and 15 touchdowns against 11 interceptions, enough to claim the AFL passing crown. His 88.2 passing rating was the highest for a rookie in the history of the league. His record would stand 15 years, until Dan Marino broke it with an incredible 96.0 in 1983. Cook's record average gain per attempt of 9.411 yards remains the highest for a rookie in league history.

All the promise that seemed so great disappeared in a flash after the 1969 season. Cook would attempt but three passes over the remainder of his career. That next season, his arm went out in preseason training, and Cook spent the rest of his career on and off injured reserve trying to rehabilitate it. His arm never recovered, and his career ended in 1974.

Gary Danielson

Gary Danielson has no stunning championship performances to show for his 10 years in the NFL. But the veteran quarterback for the Cleveland Browns has quietly worked his way to the upper levels of his craft. His career statistics rank him twentieth on the NFL's all-time rating of quarterbacks. That puts him in company with the game's greatest names. He has achieved that distinction despite never having led the league in passing in any season.

Over the years, Danielson has completed 1049 of 1847 attempts for 13,159 yards. He has thrown 77 touchdown passes and 77 interceptions and has a 75.6 rating. In 1980, Danielson set a club record in passing yardage for the Detroit Lions with 3223 yards. In 1983, when Danielson was the backup to Eric Hipple, the club went to a 9-7 record and its first NFC Central Division title in more than a decade. In the playoffs, however, Danielson threw five interceptions and the San Francisco 49ers nipped Detroit, 24-23.

In 1986, the Lions traded Danielson to Cleveland, where he sat out the season with an injury.

Above: *Greg Cook, the Bengals' rookie sensation in 1969, threw for 1854 yards and 15 touchdowns.*

Left: *Gary Danielson's 3223 passing yards set a Detroit Lions record in 1983.*

Ed Danowski

Ed Danowski gained fame in the 1930s as the quarterback who led the New York Giants to four NFL title games. On the strength of his efforts, the Giants won two championships.

The 1934 championship has gone down in history as the famous 'sneakers' game in which New York faced the original Monsters of the Midway, the Chicago Bears with Bronko Nagurski. Chicago had beaten the Giants during the regular season, and the championship game seemed a foregone conclusion as 35,000 fans at the Polo Grounds watched the Bears bulldoze to a 13-3 lead through the third quarter.

The frozen field had left the New York ground game with spinning wheels until the Giants running backs donned rubber-soled basketball shoes at halftime. Finding their traction as the third period closed, the Giants turned the game into a track meet, scoring 27 points to win 30-13. The stunned Bears seemed helpless spectators as Danowski threw 28 yards for one touchdown and ran nine yards for another.

In 1935, the Giants reached the championship game again, winning the East with a 9-3 record as Danowski led the league in passing with 794 yards. In the title game against the Detroit Lions, he threw a 42-yard touchdown pass but could muster no more offense as New York fell to Detroit, 26-7.

The 1938 team again made it to the championship game, where they beat the Packers in a 23-17 cliffhanger. Danowski had another great passing day,

throwing two touchdown passes, including the game-winner to Hank Soar in the fourth quarter.

Danowski again won the league passing title in 1939 by completing 70 of 129 passes for 848 yards, although the Packers pounded the Giants in the championship game, 27-0.

Above: *Ed Danowski of the New York Giants launches a punt in preparation for a 1934 game at the Polo Grounds.*
Left: *Danowski (22) carries the ball up the middle in the 1934 championship game against the Bears. The Giants wore sneakers to gain traction on the frozen turf and won the game, 30-13.*

Len Dawson

Len Dawson's career covered the breadth of the modern pro football experience, from journeyman duty in the NFL to three AFL championships to a Super Bowl ring to induction into the Hall of Fame in 1987.

In addition to all the team trophies, Dawson racked up some fine statistics over his 19 years as a pro. He was the AFL's top-rated passer for four years – 1962, 1964, 1966 and 1968. He also led his league a record eight seasons in the percentage of passes he completed. For another four seasons, he threw more touchdown passes than any AFL quarterback.

A 6-foot, 190-pounder, Dawson was a first-round draft pick of the Pittsburgh Steelers out of Purdue in 1957. He was traded to the Cleveland Browns for the 1960 and 1961 seasons, then wound up with the Dallas Texans of the AFL for 1962. It was there that he struck the rich vein of fame, leading the Texans to the AFL championship game by throwing for 2759 yards and 29 touchdowns, enough to earn him the AFL passing crown.

The 1962 AFL championship game was a sudden-death, double-overtime classic, pitting Dawson and the Texans against George Blanda and the Houston Oilers. Dawson passed cautiously for 88 yards and one touchdown. Then in the second overtime, he carefully worked Dallas into field position for Tommy Brooker's field goal and a 20-17 win.

The next year Dallas owner Lamar Hunt moved his team to Kansas City to become the Chiefs, where Dawson and the franchise struggled to remain above .500. Then in 1966, Dawson won another AFL passing crown, throwing for 2527 yards and 26 touchdowns as the Chiefs won the Western Division with an 11-2-1 record. In the AFL title game, Dawson completed 16 of 24 passes for 227 yards and two touchdowns, and the Chiefs rolled past Buffalo, 31-7, to play the NFL champion Green Bay Packers in Super Bowl I. As underdogs, Dawson and the Chiefs played well for a half against the Packers and trailed only 14-10. But Dawson threw a key interception early in the second half, and Green Bay rode that momentum to victory, 35-10. Dawson had completed 16 of 27 passes for 211 yards against one of pro football's legendary defenses.

Three years later Dawson and the Chiefs were back at the Super Bowl, this time as 13-point underdogs to swashbuckling Joe Kapp and the Minnesota Vikings. The Kansas City offense was bolstered by veteran placekicker Jan Stenerud. Mike Garrett gave the ground game its wheels. The defense, with Curly Culp, Buck Buchanan, Bobby Bell and Willie Lanier, was already renowned. Kansas City's offense did its work early, and Stenerud came on to kick three field goals. Coupled with Garrett's five-yard touchdown run, that gave the Chiefs a 16-0 halftime lead. Kansas

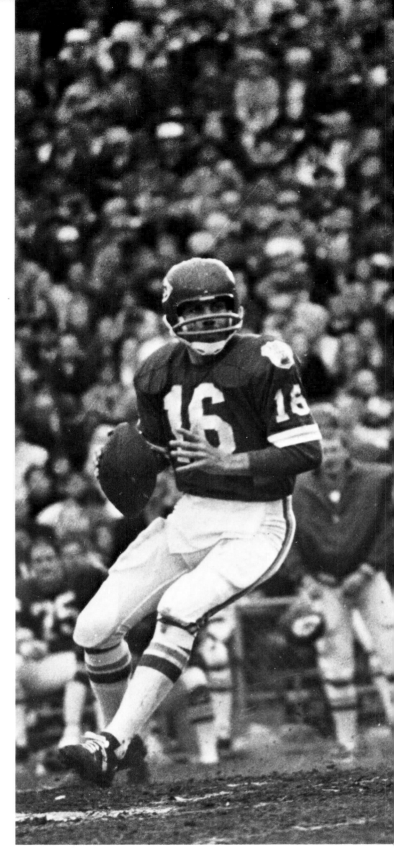

City rode defense and ball control to a 23-7 win. Dawson completed 12 of 17 passes for 142 yards, with one touchdown and one interception.

The Chiefs never returned to championship form after their magic year, but Dawson continued to combine personal style with passing accuracy. His final season, 1975, was exemplary of his career, as he again finished the year as the NFL's most accurate passer, completing a higher percentage of his attempts than any other quarterback in the league.

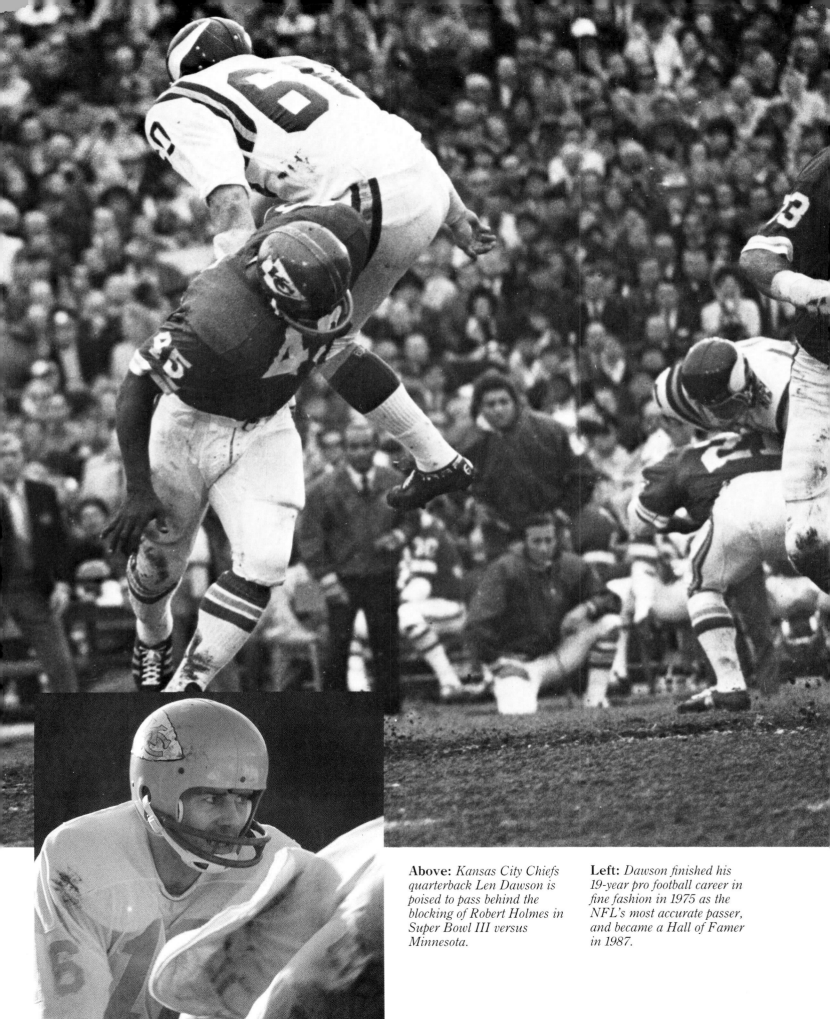

Above: *Kansas City Chiefs quarterback Len Dawson is poised to pass behind the blocking of Robert Holmes in Super Bowl III versus Minnesota.*

Left: *Dawson finished his 19-year pro football career in fine fashion in 1975 as the NFL's most accurate passer, and became a Hall of Famer in 1987.*

Steve DeBerg

In his 11 years of NFL experience, Steve DeBerg has established a reputation as one of the league's steadiest journeymen. He has a track record as the veteran who eases the adjustment of talented young quarterbacks. He was at San Francisco when Joe Montana arrived there in 1980, at Denver in 1983 to help supervise the debut of John Elway, and at Tampa Bay for the appearance of Steve Young and Vinny Testaverde. In between, DeBerg has managed to do a little playing of his own.

A San Jose State product, DeBerg threw for 7220 yards in a little over four seasons with the 49ers. When Bill Walsh arrived at San Francisco, he named DeBerg his quarterback. He responded by completing 347 of 578 attempts for 3652 yards. The 347 completions was an NFL record. The 49ers, however, struggled with a weak defense and relied almost entirely on DeBerg's arm. That one-dimensional approach resulted in a 2-14 season.

DeBerg was traded to Denver during the 1981 season, where he shared playing time. In December 1982, DeBerg set a short-lived NFL record by throwing 18 consecutive complete passes, 17 versus the LA Rams on 12 December, then one the next week against Kansas City, but Cincinnati's Ken Anderson broke it two weeks later by throwing 20 straight completions. In 1983, DeBerg alternated with rookie John Elway and played a major role in helping the Broncos to the playoffs. He was traded to Tampa Bay for the 1984 season, where he turned in one of his better pro performances, completing 308 of 509 attempts for 3554 yards and 19 touchdowns.

Used primarily as a backup in 1985-86, DeBerg opened the 1987 season with five touchdown passes as Tampa Bay demolished Atlanta. Vinny Testaverde, the 1986 Heisman trophy winner, was serving as DeBerg's understudy. And, as Testaverde told reporters, he couldn't have a better teacher.

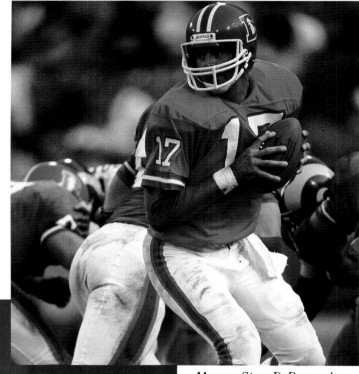

Above: *Steve DeBerg, who played for Denver from 1981-83, pivots after taking the snap.*
Left: *DeBerg set an NFL record while at San Francisco, throwing 347 completions.*
Opposite: *Lynn Dickey of the Green Bay Packers was one of the most accurate passers in the club's history.*

Lynn Dickey

Lynn Dickey's career with the Green Bay Packers went through some ups and downs as coach Bart Starr struggled to rebuild the club during the early 1980s. Despite the handicap of a weak team and a porous defense, Dickey ran up some impressive passing numbers. In 1983, he set two Packer season passing records with 4458 yards and 32 touchdown passes. That season he completed 18 consecutive passes in a September game against Houston. That achievement ties him with two other quarterbacks for the second longest string in league history. In that game against Houston, Dickey also threw five touchdown passes, tying a club record.

In 1981, Dickey quarterbacked the second most accurate game in NFL history by completing 19 of 21 passes against New Orleans, an incredible 90.48 percent completion rate. His 4458 yards passing in 1983 ranks him sixth in that category in the NFL.

Bobby Douglass

It is absurd to think of a modern pro quarterback rushing for nearly 1000 yards, but that's just what Chicago Bears signal caller Bobby Douglass did during the 1972 season.

A large left-hander from the University of Kansas, Douglass used his mobility and size to break for extra yardage. He was never better than a mediocre passer, but his double-threat in the age of the bomb makes him a stand-out among his contemporaries.

In fact, he led the Bears both in passing and rushing for 1972, gaining 968 yards on the ground in 141 attempts and passing for 1246. He ran for eight touchdowns that season and passed for nine more, as Chicago struggled to a 4-9-1 record.

He joined the Bears in 1969 and played with them for seven seasons. As a rookie he shared playing time with veteran Jack Concannon. In 1971-73, he carried Chicago's quarterbacking chores full-time. In his seven seasons with the Bears, he passed for nearly 5000 yards and 30 touchdowns. Even better, he rushed for 2470 yards and 20 touchdowns, enough to rank him ninth on the team's all-time list of ball carriers.

Paddy Driscoll

John 'Paddy' Driscoll was one of pro football's early quarterbacks. Accordingly, he made his mark as a drop-kicker, not a passer. Although backs did attempt to throw the fat football used in the game's early decades, it was a difficult and risky procedure. The throwers would cup their hands around the larger ball and sling it loosely. If an incomplete pass strayed out of bounds, the defense took over possession at the point where it went out. As a result, the pass in those early days was used more like a punt. But as a kicker, Driscoll was deadly from a 45-to 50-yard range.

A 5-foot-11, 160-pounder, he played for Northwestern in 1915 and 1916. In 1918, he joined the Great Lakes Naval Training Station squad and was teamed with George Halas and Jimmy Conzelman. That talented bunch won the 1919 Rose Bowl, and 18 months later, Driscoll joined Halas' Decatur Staleys, the forerunner of the Chicago Bears.

After the 1920 season, Driscoll shifted to the rival Chicago Cardinals and played with them for five seasons, leading them to the NFL championship in 1925 with an 11-2-1 record. Driscoll then rejoined Halas and the Bears through the 1929 season when he retired. The 1926 Bears rolled to a 12-1-3 record, but that was only good enough for second place behind the Frankford Yellow Jackets, the forerunner of the Philadelphia

Eagles. In a key game with the Jackets, Driscoll had scored but Guy Chamberlin broke through and blocked Driscoll's PAT kick to preserve Frankford's 7-6 victory. The Bears never got closer to the title during Driscoll's playing days.

A native of Evanston, Illinois, Driscoll was inducted into the Hall of Fame in 1965. He died in 1968 at the age of 72.

Tony Eason

The New England Patriots selected Tony Eason from the University of Illinois in the first round of the 1983 NFL draft. Two years later, he teamed with fellow quarterback Steve Grogan to take the Pats to the Super Bowl.

He performed with spare but deadly precision in the 1985 AFC championship game against the Miami Dolphins. In driving the Patriots to a 31-14 win, he completed 10 of 12 passes for 71 yards and three touchdowns. Prior to that, the Patriots hadn't beaten Miami in the Orange Bowl in 18 years. The Super Bowl, on the other hand, was a debacle for the Patriots, as the Chicago Bears' defense disassembled New England's offense and won, 46-10.

For 1986, Eason completed 276 of 448 attempts for 3328 yards with 19 touchdowns and only 10 interceptions, enough to give him a fine 89.2 rating on the season. His performance boosted the Patriots to another AFC Eastern Division crown with an 11-5 record. Eason injured his shoulder in a late victory over Miami but came back to push the Patriots to a 17-13 third-quarter lead with two touchdown passes against John Elway and the Denver Broncos in the playoffs. But then the Broncos found 12 points and stretched past New England, 22-17.

A 6-foot-4, 212-pounder, Eason is among a group of young NFL quarterbacks whose futures seem bright.

Opposite top: *Chicago Bears quarterback Bobby Douglass rolls for yardage. Double-threat Douglass rushed for almost 1000 yards and passed for 1246 in 1972.*
Opposite bottom: *Hall of Famer Paddy Driscoll, quarterback/drop-kicker, finished his career with George Halas and the Bears in 1929.*
Above right: *Rifler Tony Eason of the New England Patriots.*
Right: *Eason calls his variables against the Saints. The young quarterback out of Illinois threw for 3328 yards and 19 touchdowns in 1986.*

John Elway

When John Elway came out of Stanford University in 1983, the book on him cited boundless talent but questioned his moxie and consistency. His first four years with the Denver Broncos seemed to confirm that assessment. Then in the 1986 season, Elway silenced his critics by passing the Broncos to Super Bowl XXI. In the process, he contributed a great moment or two to the annals of the game.

The regular season went nicely enough. Elway completed 280 of 504 attempts for 3485 yards and 19 touchdowns against 13 interceptions. And the Broncos rolled through the schedule to win the AFC West. In the playoffs, the Broncos fell behind New England, but Elway rallied them for a 22-17 win to advance to the AFC finals against the Cleveland Browns.

Elway was hampered by an injured left ankle, and the Broncos seemed to draw on that image, limping step for step with the Browns through the chilly afternoon to a 13-13 tie in the fourth quarter. Then with just under six minutes left, Cleveland scored to give them what seemed to be an insurmountable lead, 20-13. On the ensuing kickoff the Broncos bobbled the ball and wound up on their own two-yard line, with 5:32 left. Calmly and precisely, Elway worked the Broncos to the Brown 40 with the clock showing 1:59.

Elway threw an incompletion and was sacked on the next play for an eight-yard loss. With time quickly running out, he then dropped to the shotgun, managed to control a bumbled snap and zipped the ball to Mark Jackson for a 20-yard gain to the Cleveland 28. Elway's next shot, a 14-yarder to Sewell was followed by an incompletion. So Elway broke and ran for nine yards to the five. There, on third and one he hit Jackson for the touchdown. Rich Karlis's placement tied it at 20. In overtime, Elway once more jumpstarted the Broncos and drove them down to the Brown 15, where Karlis punched up the game-winning field goal, 23-20.

The Broncos met their match in Super Bowl XXI where the New York Giants wrapped them up, 39-20. But Elway's excellent performance in the 1987 season, which took the Broncos to the Super Bowl again, indicates that he may prove to be a player for the ages.

Above: *Denver's John Elway mastered one of the greatest comebacks ever against Cleveland in the 1986 AFC Championship.*

Right: *Elway looks for a receiver in a 1986 game against Dallas.*
Opposite: *The Bengals' Boomer Esiason.*

Boomer Esiason

Among the best of the brightest in the crop of talented young NFL quarterbacks is Boomer Esiason of the Cincinnati Bengals. He's big (6-foot-4, 220 pounds), strong-armed, and mobile. Beyond that, he's a fanatical student of the game who developed under the tutelage of Coach Bobby Ross at the University of Maryland.

Esiason became the starter for the Bengals when Ken Anderson was injured after four games in the 1985 season, and despite the late start, managed to pass for 3443 yards. In 1986, he was the driving force in the NFL's most potent offense. Esiason completed 273 of 469 passes for 3959 yards and 24 touchdowns against 17 interceptions. In the final regular-season game against the New York Jets, Esiason passed for 425 yards and five touchdowns, as Cincinnati won, 52-21. The Bengals ripped off a 10-6 record, their first winning season since 1982. Esiason was rewarded for his performance by being named to the Pro Bowl at the season's end.

Joe Ferguson

Joe Ferguson came to the Buffalo Bills in 1973 out of the University of Arkansas, where he had guided the Razorbacks to a Top 20 ranking in the college polls.

In 1987, Ferguson headed into his fifteenth season in the NFL as a backup quarterback for the Detroit Lions. Yet in his heyday, he was nothing but 'Front Row Joe,' one of the league's top-flight talents. He ranks tenth on the NFL's all-time list for career passing attempts with 4375 and eleventh on the completion list with 2292. In total yardage he ranks twelfth on the all-time list with 28,895 yards. He holds the eighteenth spot in touchdown passes with 190.

His performance translated into team success for the Bills, who had languished at the bottom of the standings in the AFC East. They finished 9-5 in 1973, his first year. The next season they also finished 9-5, only this time it earned them a wild card playoff berth. The Bills lost to Super Bowl-bound Pittsburgh, 32-14, in the first round.

Their fortunes sagged again through the rest of the decade. But in 1980, Ferguson found his form and paced them to the division title with an 11-5 record. They lost to San Diego and 'Air Coryell' in the playoffs, 20-14. But Ferguson came back in 1981 to set a team record for passing yardage with 3652. That helped translate into a 10-6 record and a wild card slot for the playoffs, where Buffalo jumped the Jets, 31-27. In the next round, they lost a heartbreaker to Cincinnati, 28-21. In 1983, Ferguson set another club record, for touchdown passes, with 26 on the season, but the Bills broke even on the season at 8-8.

The championship magic has eluded Ferguson over the years, as it has many other great quarterbacks who have labored for incomplete teams. But like many of the other greats, Ferguson certainly has a good measure of staying power and longevity. He may just hang around the league long enough to step into the warm light of opportunity.

28

Vince Ferragamo

Vince Ferragamo's best years by far were in Los Angeles, where he led the Rams to Super Bowl XIV.

In 1979, the Rams were struggling early in the season, with quarterback Pat Haden injured and Ferragamo out with a broken left hand. Ferragamo returned to the lineup to lead the team to victory in six of seven games, pushing their record to 9-7 and giving them their seventh consecutive Western Division title. While LA had consistently dominated the division standings, the club always broke down in the playoffs. Ferragamo changed that in 1979, pushing his mates past Dallas, 21-19, in the first round, then taking the NFC crown with a 9-0 win over Tampa Bay.

The Rams faced the Pittsburgh Steelers and their fearsome defense in Super Bowl XIV. Ferragamo's performance was gutsy, connecting on 15 of 25 attempts for 212 yards, enough to push LA to a surprising 19-17 third-quarter lead. The Steelers, however, gained their footing early in the fourth quarter and drove for a touchdown and a 24-19 lead. Ferragamo then made his only mistake of the day,

throwing a pass that was picked off by Steelers linebacker Jack Lambert. It cost them the game.

The next season, Ferragamo set a Rams club record by throwing 30 touchdown passes. The Rams improved their record to 11-5, but that was only good enough for second place in the division and a wild card in the playoffs, where they lost to Dallas, 34-13, in the first round. In the strike-shortened 1982 season, Vince passed for 509 yards against Chicago, the third highest single-game total in league history. In 1983, Ferragamo set another Rams passing record by throwing for 3276 yards. His team's 9-7 record was good for another wild card in the playoffs. This time the Rams beat Dallas, 24-17, in the first round only to stumble into a disaster in the next game, losing to the Redskins, 51-7.

Ferragamo never got the opportunity to return to the Super Bowl, as his career shifted from contract disputes to a stint in the Canadian Football League. Yet in his hour in 1979, he showed the football world he had what it takes to challenge the best.

Opposite left: *Joe Ferguson has carried the Buffalo Bills to some of their more successful seasons.*
Opposite right: *Ferguson unleashes a pass amidst a Bronco rush.*
Left: *Vince Ferragamo of the Los Angeles Rams looks over his offensive line.*

Frank Filchock

For six years Frank Filchock was a backup quarterback to Washington's legendary Sammy Baugh. His distinction in the league came from a record 99-yard championship pass to Andy Farkas against Pittsburgh in October 1939.

Things changed with the 1945 NFL championship when Filchock replaced Baugh, who was injured and struggling. There, in the chill winds of Cleveland's Municipal Stadium, Filchock showed the sports world his stuff, throwing two touchdown passes to match the powerful Cleveland Rams punch for punch. Only a first-quarter safety, scored on a freak rule and a Baugh pass, gave Cleveland a 15-14 edge. Twice in the last quarter, Filchock drove the Redskins into field goal position, only to see the gusting winds carry the kick awry. With the weather helping them on defense, the Rams claimed the title, 15-14.

Before the next season, Filchock was traded to the New York Giants. He responded by driving the Giants to a 7-3-1 record and a spot facing the Chicago Bears in the 1947 NFL championship game. Then, the day before the game, news broke that a professional gambler, Alvin Paris, had offered $2500 bribes to Filchock and New York fullback Merle Hapes. Hapes was not allowed to play because he acknowledged the incident. Filchock, however, denied involvement and was allowed to play.

He took the field that day to boos from the home crowd at New York's Polo Grounds. Filchock suffered a broken nose as Chicago took a 14-0 lead, but he shook off the injury and threw two touchdown passes to tie the game at 14 in the third quarter. Despite Filchock's efforts, the Bears won the championship with 10 points in the fourth quarter.

He was suspended after the season for his part in the scandal. His suspension lifted in 1950, Filchock joined the Baltimore Colts but played sparingly. His youth and ability had flown. Filchock's legacy hung on the fact that for two years in a row, for two teams, he had shown his mettle in the championship game.

Left: *Quarterback Frank Filchock played for the Redskins, Giants, and Colts during his NFL tenure.*
Opposite top: *Tom Flores, Oakland Raiders signal-caller from 1960 to 1966 and then Raiders coach until the end of the 1987 season.*
Opposite bottom: *Flores scans his receivers downfield in a game against the Jets. He threw for 407 yards and six touchdowns against Houston in 1963.*

Tom Flores

Tom Flores broke most of Eddie LeBaron's records at the University of the Pacific in the late 1950s, and joined the Oakland Raiders in 1960. In 1963, Al Davis joined Oakland as coach, and the team's fortunes experienced an upswing. Coming back from injury, Flores led the team to eight wins on the way to a 10-4 record. In a 22 December home game with Houston, Flores completed 17 of 29 passes for 407 yards and six touchdowns. George Blanda threw five touchdowns, but Flores won one of the wildest shootouts in pro football history, 52-49.

In six seasons with the Raiders, he completed 810 of 1640 attempts for 11,635 yards and an incredible 92 touchdowns. His best season was 1966 with 2638 yards and 24 touchdowns. He was then traded to Buffalo in a move that brought Daryle Lamonica to Oakland. He finished his career as a backup to Len Dawson at Kansas City, where he earned a Super Bowl ring when the Chiefs beat the Minnesota Vikings in Super Bowl IV.

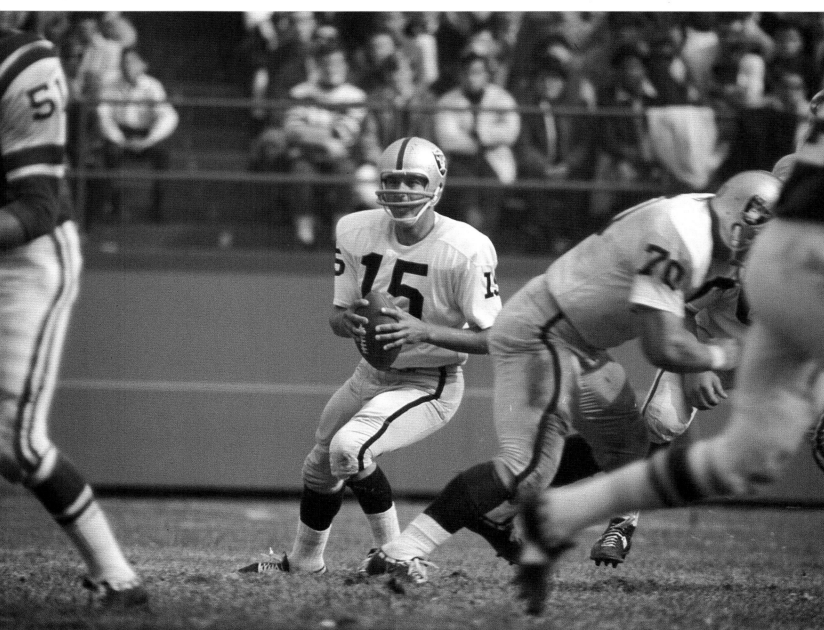

Dan Fouts

A third-round draft pick out of the University of Oregon, Dan Fouts entered the NFL in 1973. But it would be six seasons before his career would take off in 1979, when Don Coryell became coach of the San Diego Chargers and created the passing phenomenon dubbed 'Air Coryell.'

The 6-foot-3 Fouts would be Coryell's pilot, taking the Chargers' air game to new heights and new records while leading the league in passing for four straight seasons. In 1979, he passed for 4082 yards, including an unheard-of four straight games with more than 300 yards passing each. His superb performance lifted the Chargers to the AFC West title with a 12-4 record. San Diego was ousted by the Houston Oilers in the playoffs, 17-14, but they bounced right back into the jet stream the next season.

In 1980, Fouts connected with his talented wing-mates, wide receivers John Jefferson and Charlie Joiner and tight end Kellen Winslow, to better the record to 4715 yards, and again the Chargers claimed the AFC West title, this time with an 11-5 record. In eight games in 1980, Fouts struck for more than 300 yards, and the Chargers bolted to the AFC title game against the Oakland Raiders. Fouts' highlights included a 50-yard bomb with 2:08 left in the playoff battle with Buffalo to give San Diego a 20-14 come-from-behind win. Highly favored against the Raiders, the Chargers fell behind 28-7 in the second quarter and fought their way back only to lose, 34-28.

The yardage meter jumped even higher in 1981, to 4802 yards, as Fouts set a record for passing attempts in a season (609) and the Chargers claimed a third Western crown with a 10-6 record. Again, they shot their way to the playoffs, where Fouts and Winslow put together an overtime classic, a 41-38 win over Miami. Unfortunately, the AFC championship game at Cincinnati was played in freezing conditions, and the Bengals killed Fouts' last great chance at the Super Bowl with a 28-7 victory.

From there, the players' strike shortened the 1982 season, Air Coryell fell from the skies and never really got close to playoff contention again. Nevertheless, Fouts has fought off injuries to remain the whirlwind of talent at the center of San Diego's hopes.

Above: *San Diego's Dan Fouts runs for an 11-yard gain, with the Raiders' John Matuszak hot on his trail.*
Opposite: *LA's Roman Gabriel throws one of four TD passes in a 42-14 win over the 49ers.*

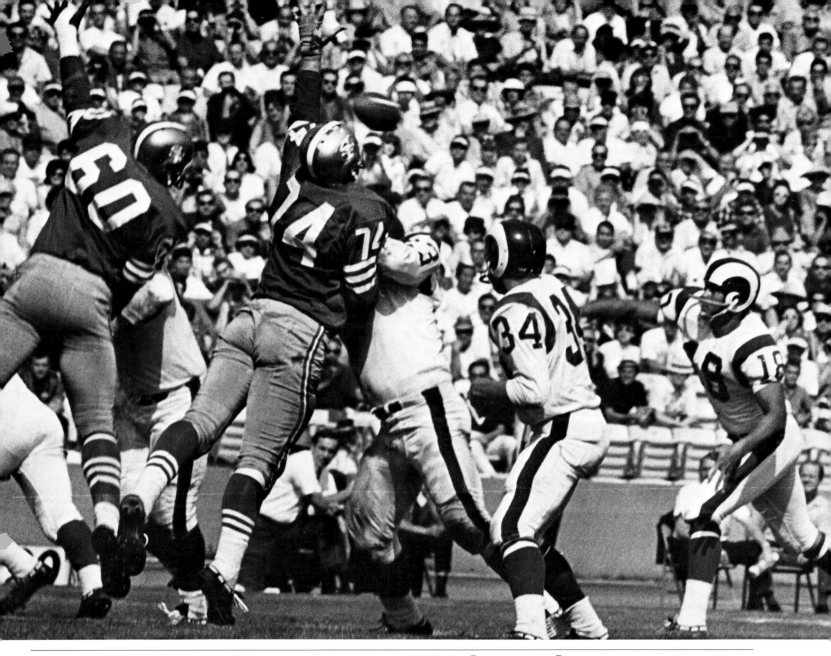

Roman Gabriel

In 1962, the Los Angeles Rams made North Carolina State quarterback Roman Gabriel the top player selected in the draft. The Rams were cellar dwellers until 1966, when the team's owners hired coach George Allen, and suddenly they were able to take on the best in the league.

On their way to an 11-1 season and a divisional crown in 1967, the Rams met the defending world champions, the Green Bay Packers, in a crucial December game. Their collision would go down as one of the greatest battles in league history. One of the stars of the show was Gabriel, who completed 20 of 36 passes for 227 yards and three touchdowns against what was perhaps pro football's greatest defense. His last touchdown pass, a six-yarder, came with 37 seconds left and gave Los Angeles a 27-24 win. Green Bay would gain revenge in the first round of the playoffs, beating the Rams, 28-7. Still, the NFL had been served notice that

the Rams would no longer linger at the bottom of the standings.

Over the next two years, Gabriel gained a reputation as one of the NFL's most accurate passers. Over the 1968 and 1969 seasons, he threw 206 passes without an interception, the third longest stretch in the history of the league. Gabriel drove the Rams to the division crown again in 1969, with an 11-3 record. LA lost to Minnesota, 23-20, in the first round, and Gabriel never gained a championship appearance.

He did, however, run up a prodigious passing record over the course of his career. He holds the Rams' club career passing records for yards (22,223) and touchdown passes (154), as well as NFL all-time career ratings of twelfth place for touchdown passes (201), sixth place for passes attempted (4498), ninth place for completions (2366) and eleventh place for yards passing (29,444).

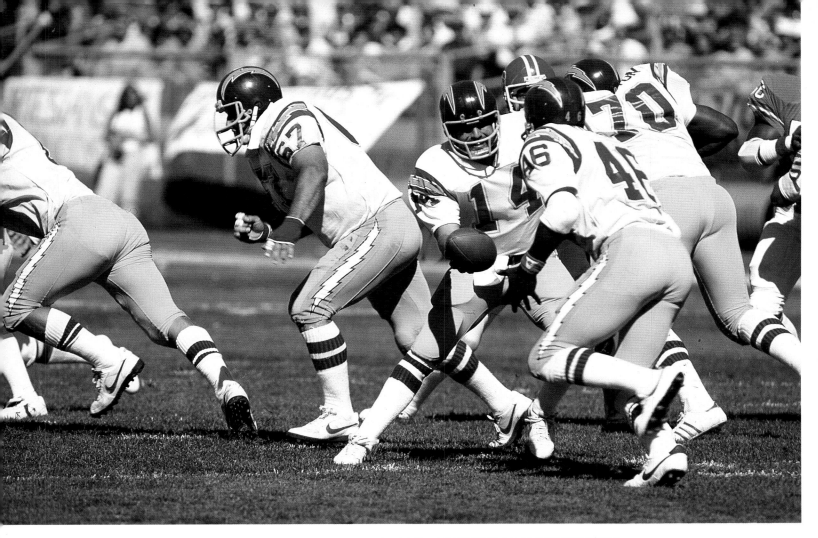

Above: *Chargers quarterback Dan Fouts, shown here about to hand off, led the NFL in passing for four consecutive seasons.*
Left: *Roman Gabriel took snaps for the Philadelphia Eagles later in his career.*
Opposite: *Gabriel threw 201 touchdown passes, 4498 attempted passes, 2366 completions, and covered a total of 29,444 yards in his NFL career.*

Otto Graham

The All-America Football Conference began in 1946 as a rival to the NFL. The upstart league would eventually be recognized for bringing great players and teams to pro football. Among the very best was Cleveland Browns quarterback Otto Graham.

Paul Brown of Ohio State coaching fame was 36 and still in the service when he was hired as coach of the new AAFC team, the Cleveland Browns. His first act as Browns coach was to seek out the services of Graham, another serviceman who had been a utility tailback of sorts at Northwestern University from 1941-43. Graham mostly ran and blocked for Northwestern, but Brown had recognized his strong passing arm and admired his ability. Around Graham, Brown built an efficient, powerful team, with Dante Lavelli and Mac Speedie as lightning receivers and Marion Motley and Ray Renfro as running backs.

Brown believed heartily in the passing game and directed his attentions to perfecting a great one. His major innovation was the shifting of the offense from a simple man-to-man to a complicated attack with multiple receivers. In Graham, Speedie, Lavelli and Motley, he had the ideal ingredients. The results were terrifying, nearly fatal, to the rest of the AAFC. In the four years of the league's existence, the Browns won all four championships, compiling a record of 52 wins, four losses and two ties. In each of the 1947, 1948, and 1949 seasons, Graham passed for more than 2700 yards, far more than any other quarterback had totalled in a three-year period.

In 1949 NFL Commissioner Bert Bell announced the merger of the two leagues for the 1950 season. From the eight AAFC teams, only three – the Browns, the Baltimore Colts, and the San Francisco 49ers – survived in the NFL. Yet their competitive effect would be felt almost immediately.

In the first game of the 1950 season, the Browns met the defending NFL champions, the Philadelphia Eagles. In all fairness, Philadelphia was hurting, with back Steve Van Buren out with a foot injury. Yet the

Right: *Otto Graham and his Cleveland Browns teammates are all smiles after pounding the Detroit Lions 56-10 for the 1954 title.*
Below: *Hall of Famer Graham led the league in pass completion percentage from 1953 to 1955.*

Opposite: *Graham crosses the goal line for one of his three rushing touchdowns on 28 December 1954. He passed for three more TDs to win the title in high style for the Browns.*

Browns' 35-10 victory was decisive. Graham completed 21 of 38 passes for 310 yards and three touchdowns. The Browns went on to win the American Conference with a 10-2 record and blew past the New York Giants, 8-3, to face Los Angeles for the crown on Christmas Eve.

Some, including Commissioner Bell, have argued that the 1950 NFL Championship was the greatest ever played. In all, six records would be set and three others tied. On the first offensive play, LA quarterback Bob Waterfield threw an 82-yard touchdown pass. Graham answered with a scoring pass for Cleveland and the race was on. LA led at the half, 14-13.

When Cleveland's Marion Motley fumbled on the Browns six in the second half, Larry Brink picked up the ball and ran it in for a 28-20 Rams lead. Graham threw a TD pass to bring the score to 28-27. Then he guided a late drive to the LA 10, where Lou Groza kicked a field goal with 20 seconds left for a 30-28 win and the championship.

For 1951, Graham again drove the Browns to the NFL title game, only to lose to Los Angeles, 24-17. For 1952, Cleveland and Graham continued their mastery of the NFL's American Conference, but lost the 1952 championship to a new power in the National Conference, the Detroit Lions. In 1953 the Browns won their first 11 games, including a 62-14 humiliation of the rival New York Giants, and claimed the divisional title handily. But again, the Lions slipped away with the NFL title, 17-16.

The next season, Cleveland settled the rubber match by soundly thumping the favored Lions, 56-10, for the 1954 championship. Graham, who had passed for more than 2700 yards during the season, had announced his retirement before the game. But after he passed for 163 yards and ran for three touchdowns on the title game, he changed his mind.

It was a good decision. The 1955 season was all Graham. The Browns returned to the championship to meet the Rams, who had been led there by Norm Van Brocklin's 2637 yards passing. A crowd of 85,693 crammed into Los Angeles Coliseum and saw Graham complete 14 of 25 passes for 202 yards and two touchdowns. He ran two other scores across. A 38-14 win and another championship brought the perfect ending to Graham's playing career. He had led the league by completing the highest percentage of passes in 1953, 1954 and 1955. His 99.1 passing rating for 1953 and a 94.1 rating for 1955 rank him among the NFL's all-time greats. He was inducted into the Hall of Fame in 1965.

Bob Griese

In 1967, the Miami Dolphins snapped up Purdue quarterback Bob Griese in the first round of the AFL draft. He and the young franchise struggled until 1970 when Don Shula became the team's head coach. From there the fortunes of the player and the team zoomed off at a meteoric rate.

The Dolphins and Griese capped off an astounding 1971 season by sneaking past the Kansas City Chiefs in a Christmas Day playoff battle, the longest game in NFL history. Griese played despite a painfully injured left shoulder. The game was a kicking duel pitting Miami's Garo Yepremian against KC's Jan Stenerud. Griese was left with the duty of getting the ball close enough to let Yepremian use his toe. After six periods of play and two sudden-death overtimes, the game came down to a photo finish with the Dolphins the victors, 27-24.

The next week Griese was precise in driving the Dolphins past Johnny Unitas and the Baltimore Colts in the AFC championship, 21-0. The Super Bowl, however, was a game too far. Shula's bunch had spent most of their magic. The Cowboys, behind Staubach's precision passing, dispatched the Dolphins, 24-3.

For 1972 the Dolphins were geared for total victory, led by the intensity of Griese and Coach Shula and fortified by the backfield of Larry Csonka, Mercury Morris and Jim Kiick. Before the season was out, the Dolphins would dispatch 17 opponents in a row for the NFL's only perfect season. Griese broke an ankle mid-season and had to be replaced by 38-year-old Earl Morrall, but was back in time for the Super Bowl, versus the Washington Redskins.

The game, played before 90,000 at Memorial Coliseum in Los Angeles, was controlled by Miami's efficiency. Miami scored in each of the first two quarters, allowed a second half score off a recovery of Garo Yepremian's fumble, then settled in for a dominating 14-7 victory.

For 1973, the Miami Dolphins fell short of another perfect season (they finished 12-2), but they still topped off the year by beating the Minnesota Vikings in Super Bowl VIII. Griese completed six of seven pass attempts and ran the offense to perfection. Larry Csonka rushed for 145 yards, as the Dolphins bulled to a 24-0 third-quarter lead, and coasted to the win, 24-7.

It seemed the Dolphins might dominate for years to come, but a glitch developed in the grand scheme of things. The World Football League held its organizational meeting the day after the Super Bowl, and by March the Toronto Northmen of the new league had signed Csonka, Kiick and Paul Warfield to contracts. Although Csonka and Warfield played with the Dolphins in 1974, the championship atmosphere had been shattered. The WFL completed one season, then gasped and died in the middle of the next, surviving just long enough to dismantle one of pro football's truly great teams.

Griese remained with Shula and the Dolphins through the 1980 season, after which he retired. In his 14 years with Miami, the Dolphins won two Super Bowls, three AFC championships, and five divisional titles. Another four times they finished second in their division.

In acknowledgment of his vital role in that success, Griese was named to the Pro Bowl six times. During his career, he passed for 25,092 yards and 192 touchdowns. He was the NFL's top-rated passer in 1971 with 2089 yards and 19 touchdowns against only nine interceptions. In 1977, he led the AFC in passing with 2252 yards and 22 touchdowns.

Left: *Miami's Bob Griese led the Dolphins to two Super Bowl victories, in 1972 and 1973, and several AFC championships.*
Opposite top left: *Griese represented the Dolphins in six Pro Bowls.*

Opposite top right: *New England's Steve Grogan has thrown for over 22,557 yards and 155 touchdowns while playing for the Patriots.*
Opposite bottom left: *LA Ram Pat Haden follows through on a long bomb.*

Above: *Pat Haden played for the Rams from 1976 to 1981, and was a Pro Bowler in 1978.*

39

Steve Grogan

The New England Patriots selected Kansas State quarterback Steve Grogan in the fifth round of the 1975 draft, and over the next decade he would throw for more touchdown passes (155) and yardage (22,557) than any player in team history.

A rangy, 6-foot-4, 210-pounder, Grogan had a rocket for an arm and a munitions dump for a temper. His explosions and frustrations became well-known throughout the league. By his second year in the league, he hustled the team to an 11-5 record and a wild card playoff spot. The Pats lost to eventual Super Bowl champion Oakland, 24-21, in the first round of the playoffs, when the Raiders scored two fourth-quarter touchdowns to come from behind. In 1978, New England with Grogan at the helm won the AFC East crown with an 11-5 record but lost to Houston, 31-14, in the first round of the playoffs.

Grogan didn't learn to control his temper until late in his career, but it came just in time to help his team to a Super Bowl. By 1985, he was a backup for the Patriots, with the young Tony Eason in the starting slot. By the third game of the season, the Patriots were 2-3 and Eason was injured. Grogan stepped in and led New England to four straight victories. Grogan had a legendary grittiness for waiting to the last second to pass just as defensive linemen crashed in on him. Using that patience, he shrugged off a sore right elbow to put the Pats back on track until Eason returned.

Asked about his role in New England's drive, Grogan told reporters, 'Defense wins championships. Quarterbacks only keep championships from being lost.' His comments would be prophetic as New England faced the awesome defense of the Chicago Bears in Super Bowl XX and lost, 46-10. Eason started the Super Bowl but Grogan was needed in relief. However, the point of the season, at least for New England, was that the talented veteran had finally conquered himself.

Pat Haden

A star at Southern Cal, Pat Haden made his first pro appearance with the Los Angeles Rams in 1976 by making his second passing attempt a 48-yard touchdown pass. Haden shared time with James Harris to lead the Rams to the NFC's Western Division title with a 10-3-1 record. In the playoffs, he and the Rams finessed the Dallas Cowboys, 14-12, to gain the NFC championship game against the Minnesota Vikings. But, unfortunately, Haden had an off day in the eight-degree weather, completing nine of 22 passing attempts for one touchdown and two interceptions, and the Rams lost 24-13.

In 1977, Haden again quarterbacked the Rams to the divisional crown with a 10-4 record, only to see his team fall in the playoffs, 14-7, again to Minnesota. The next year, with Haden again at quarterback, the Rams won their division at 12-4, then finally thumped Minnesota in the playoffs, 34-10. The NFC championship game, however, again proved Haden's undoing. Against the Dallas Cowboys, he completed only seven of 19 passes for 78 yards. Even worse, he threw three interceptions as Dallas won, 28-0.

He was named to the 1978 Pro Bowl, where his second-half passing helped the NFC to a 14-13 victory. Known more for his scrambling and a cerebral approach to the game rather than for raw talent, Haden remained with the Rams, fighting off injuries and enduring a challenge for playing time until 1981, when he retired.

John Hadl

John Hadl enjoyed a long, productive pro career covering 16 seasons and four franchises. The bulk of his duty came with the San Diego Chargers from 1962 to 1972.

He ranks fifth on the all-time list of passes attempted at 4687. He completed 2363 of them, enough to place him tenth on the all-time completions list. A high percentage of them were winners, as he holds the fourth-place spot in the all-time rankings for touchdown passes with 244. Hadl also has the fifth highest career passing yardage figures with 33,503.

For three seasons – 1965, 1968, and 1971 – Hadl led the league in yardage gained. The 1967 season also saw him lead the league in interceptions with 32. But his 1965 performance carried the Chargers to the AFL Western Division title with a 9-3-2 record. Once in the AFL title game, the Chargers were shut out, 23-0, by the Buffalo Bills. Hadl finished his career in 1977 with the Houston Oilers.

Parker Hall

Parker Hall lived out the glory dream of all footballers for two seasons, 1938 and 1939. In 1938, his senior season at the University of Mississippi, Hall led the team in passing, rushing and punting and was named a consensus All American and a member of the Chicago All-Star team of collegians.

The Cleveland Rams selected him in the first round of the 1939 draft. That fall, he turned in the performance of his career, earning an incredible slate of honors – the NFL's Most Valuable Player award, Rookie of the Year and All-Pro selection.

As a rookie, he became the third 1000-yard passer in the history of the league. Hall's 1227 yards passing in 1939 came within a hair of breaking the record set by Green Bay's Arnie Herber in 1936. The performance was enough to earn Hall the league passing crown (he also threw nine touchdown passes and 13 interceptions). To go with his arm, Hall also had a good foot. He led the league in punting his rookie year with a 40.8 yard average for 58 kicks. His longest was 80 yards.

Hall never again equalled his rookie performance, although he did set another league record in 1942, when he threw seven interceptions against the Green Bay Packers. Soon after that, however, he entered the service, and after World War II, he played only briefly before retiring.

Left: *San Diego Charger John Hadl releases a pass against the Giants on 7 November 1971. He threw 244 career TD passes.*

Above: *Parker Hall of the Cleveland Rams, the NFL MVP his rookie season, jumps up to pass in preparation for the 1940 season.*

James Harris

Quarterback James Harris twice drove the Los Angeles Rams to the threshold of the Super Bowl, and both times they were turned away.

In 1974, Harris ran the Rams to the Western Division crown with a 10-4 record. In the playoffs against the wild card Washington Redskins, they controlled the game, 19-10. In the NFC championship game against Minnesota, the Rams were trailing 7-3 in the second half when Harris drove them down to the Vikings goal, only to see an offsides set them back to the five. On the next play, a Harris pass was intercepted. He later passed for a touchdown, but the earlier lost opportunity allowed Minnesota to advance, 14-10.

In the Pro Bowl that January, Harris was named MVP when he threw two fourth-quarter touchdown passes to give the NFC a 17-10 victory. That momentum carried into the 1975 season, where Harris again drove the Rams through a 12-2 season and a Western Division crown to the verge of the Super Bowl. In the first round of the playoffs, Harris motored LA past Jim Hart and St Louis, 35-23. But in the NFC championship game against the Dallas Cowboys, Harris threw an early interception and was knocked out of the game by injuries. His replacement, Ron Jaworksi, also struggled against the fearsome Dallas defense, and the Cowboys won it, 37-7.

What was perhaps Harris' greatest performance came on 3 October 1976 against the Miami Dolphins when he completed 17 of 29 passing attempts for 436 yards and two touchdowns. Although he was hampered much of the 1976 season by a broken thumb, he still finished the year as the NFC's top-rated passer, completing 91 of 158 attempts for 1460 yards and eight touchdowns.

A Grambling alumnus, Harris was known for his strong arm, a double-edged sword of sorts in that his passes often blazed into and through receivers' hands. In 1977, Harris was traded to San Diego, where he finished his career as a backup to Dan Fouts. He retired after the 1979 season.

Jim Hart

For more than a decade, the arm of quarterback Jim Hart was the franchise for the St Louis Cardinals. A product of Southern Illinois University, he joined the team in 1966 and remained in St Louis until 1984, when he moved to the Washington Redskins, where he played a season as backup to Joe Theismann. Over the years, Hart ran up some of the best passing numbers in the history of the game. He ranks fourth on the all-time list of passes attempted (5076); fifth for passes completed (2593); eleventh in touchdown passes (209) and fourth in passing yardage (34,665).

In 1974, he led the Cardinals to the Eastern Division crown with a 10-4 record, but they lost to Minnesota in the first round of the playoffs, 30-14. The next year, Hart and his teammates bettered their record to 11-3 and again won the Eastern Division. But again they lost in the first round of the playoffs, 35-23, to the LA Rams.

Hart was named to the Pro Bowl four times – 1975, 1976, 1977, and 1978. He holds the St Louis club records for career yardage and touchdown passes. Hart retired after the 1984 season with Washington.

Opposite: *James Harris of the Los Angeles Rams fades back to fire a bullet. Harris guided the Rams to two NFC championships.*

Right: *Jim Hart quarterbacked in St Louis from 1966 to 1984. He set career yardage and TD pass records for the Cards.*

Arnie Herber

A local boy from Green Bay's West High, Arnie Herber had distinguished himself while playing at the University of Wisconsin and Regis College. He made his first appearance with the Green Bay Packers against the Chicago Cardinals early in the 1930 season and threw a touchdown pass. After that, it was hard for Coach Curly Lambeau to keep his young passer out of the lineup as Herber helped the Packers to the title in 1930 and 1931. As he matured, he developed as the league's first great passer. He led the league in that category in 1932, 1934 and 1936. In fact, his performance in 1936 marked the dawning of the NFL's great age of passers. He turned in the league's first 1000-yard performance. In 12 games, he completed 77 of 173 attempts for 1239 yards.

His throwing was matched with a record-setting receiver. Green Bay's Don Hutson, 'the Alabama Antelope,' caught 34 passes for 536 yards in 1936. His and Herber's performances returned Curly Lambeau's Packers to the NFL title game with a 10-1-1 record. Their opponents were George Marshall's Boston Redskins. At New York's Polo Grounds a crowd of 29,545 saw the Herber-Hutson combination dispatch the Redskins, 21-6. Herber passed for two touchdowns.

He again took the Packers to the title game in 1938 but saw Green Bay lose to the New York Giants, 23-17. The next year, Green Bay returned to the championship game and again faced the Giants. But after throwing the Packers' first touchdown pass, Herber gave way to Lambeau's next sensational young quarterback, Cecil Isbell.

Herber retired after the 1940 season but returned to the game in 1944 when team rosters were depleted by World War II. Despite his age, Herber quarterbacked the New York Giants to the NFL title game, but they

were beaten there by his old team, the Packers, 14-7. He retired in 1945, and his contributions to the game were recognized in 1966 with his induction into the Hall of Fame.

Cecil Isbell

Green Bay Packer quarterback Cecil Isbell made his presence known in the 1939 NFL title game. His 31-yard touchdown pass in the third quarter opened up a tight game and sent the Packers on to a 27-0 victory over the New York Giants at the State Fair Park in Milwaukee.

From that beginning, Isbell went on to lead the NFL in passing in 1941 and 1942, leaving broken records in his wake. For 1941, he completed 117 of 206 attempts for 1479 yards, a new league record. His 15 touchdown passes were also a record. Both lasted only until the next season when Isbell achieved the unfathomable, a 2000-yard passing season, by completing 146 of 268

attempts for 2021 yards. He threw 24 touchdown passes, becoming the first pro quarterback to throw for more than 20 in a season.

His 1941 Packers finished 10-1 and a tie with the great Chicago Bears for the Western Division championship. In the first divisional playoff in league history, the Bears eliminated Isbell's team, 33-14, and advanced to the NFL title game, where they humbled the New York Giants, 37-9.

Green Bay finished 8-2-1 in 1942, in second place behind the undefeated Bears in the Western Division. Isbell retired after that season to take a coaching job at his alma mater, Purdue.

Ron Jaworski

Ron Jaworski came out of Youngstown State in the 1973 NFL draft and found a spot as a backup quarterback with the Los Angeles Rams. Then in 1977 he was traded to the Philadelphia Eagles, where he teamed with Coach Dick Vermeil to bring the franchise some of its best years.

In 1978, Jaworski drove the Eagles to a 9-7 record and a wild card playoff spot. Their trip to the Super Bowl ended early, when Atlanta beat them 14-13 in the first round. The next year, Jaworski and the Eagles ran their record to 11-5, good for another wild card spot. But that, too, was ended early, 24-17, by Tampa Bay.

For 1980, Jaworski was the highest-rated passer in the NFC, completing 257 of 451 attempts for 3529 yards and 27 touchdowns against 12 interceptions. That was good enough to spur the Eagles to a 12-4 record and the Eastern Division crown. In the first round of the playoffs, they nailed Minnesota, 31-16. In the NFC championship game, Jaworski completed only nine of 29 passing attempts and threw two interceptions. But the Eagles relied on their ground game and defense to defeat the Dallas Cowboys, 20-7, and claim the NFC championship. Their opponents in Super Bowl XV were the streaking Oakland Raiders with Jim Plunkett.

In the Louisiana Superdome, Jaworski completed 18 of 38 attempts for 291 yards and a touchdown. But he was rushed hard by the Oakland defensive line and threw three interceptions as the Raiders won, 27-10. Still, Jaworski was named player of the year in the

NFC. His career statistics rank him among the best in the history of pro football. For four seasons, he passed for more than 3000 yards. Going into the 1987 season, he ranked thirteenth on the all-time list for passes attempted (4042) and fourteenth on the list for completions (2142).

Opposite: *Arnie Herber of the Green Bay Packers teamed with receiver Don Hutson to create a lethal combination for the Packers in the 1930s.*
Above: *Philadelphia's Ron Jaworski during practice. He* *and his Eagles teammates had just settled with management after the 1982 strike.*
Below: *Cecil Isbell rambles up the middle for the Packers in their 1939 27-0 victory over the Giants.*

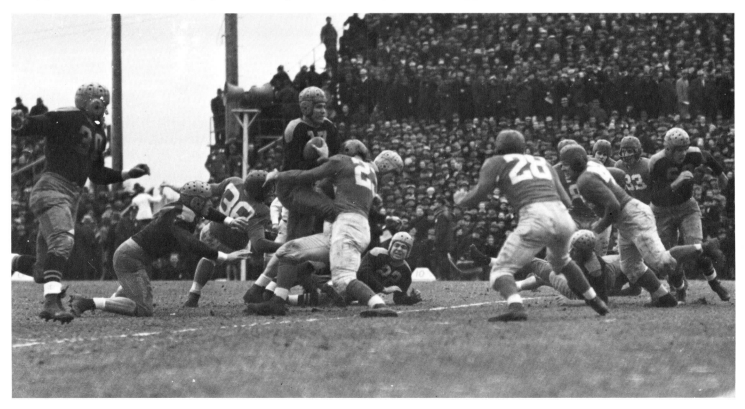

Charley Johnson

Charley Johnson came out of New Mexico State in 1961 and had an almost immediate impact on the struggling St Louis Cardinals. The Cards were just out of the league cellar for 1962, but Johnson had a great season in 1963 and pushed them to a respectable 9-5 record. He completed 222 of 423 attempts for 3280 yards and 28 touchdowns, both then club records. On 13 October, he completed 20 of 41 passes for 428 yards and two touchdowns against the Pittsburgh Steelers.

For 1964, he completed 223 of 420 attempts for 3045 yards and 21 touchdowns as the Cards ran to a 9-3-2 record. He passed for another 2400 yards in 1965, but the team finished with a losing record. The Cards returned to their winning ways in 1966, when Johnson passed for 1334 yards and 10 touchdowns, only to be interrupted by a call for military duty. He was replaced in the lineup by rookie Jim Hart. Johnson returned in 1969 to share playing time with Hart, then was traded to Houston for quarterback Pete Beathard in 1970.

He ended his career playing for Denver, where in a 18 November 1974 game against Kansas City, he completed 28 of 42 passes for 445 yards and two touchdowns. In 1976, the NFL rated its great passers of all time and ranked Johnson twenty-sixth on the list with a career rating of 69.3

Left: *St Louis' Charley Johnson threw for 222 completions, 3280 yards, and 28 touchdowns in 1963.*
Top: *LSU graduate Bert Jones went to the Baltimore Colts in 1973 and helped rebuild their program.*

Above: *Jones shows the passing form which enabled him to throw for 18,190 yards and 124 TDs in 10 pro years.*
Opposite: *Redskins warrior Sonny Jurgensen ranks seventh on the NFL's all-time passing list.*

Bert Jones

The Baltimore Colts fell on hard times in the late 1960s and early 1970s, until they selected LSU quarterback Bert Jones in the first round of the 1973 draft. From there, their fortunes improved, particularly in 1975 when Ted Marchibroda became head coach. Jones had confirmed his talent during the 1974 season, although the Colts finished 2-12 at the bottom of the AFC Eastern Division standings. That December, the young quarterback wrote his name in the record books by completing 17 consecutive passes against the New York Jets. The next season he was a major factor in a complete reversal of the Colts' fortunes, leading them to a 10-4 record and the division title, although in the playoffs they were ejected by the Pittsburgh Steelers, 28-10.

For 1976, Jones had one of the finest passing seasons in the history of the league, earning a whopping 102.6 on the league's rating scale, usually good enough to capture the league passing crown. But Oakland's Ken Stabler turned in a 103.7 season, the league's top rating. Jones' performance translated into an 11-3 season and another division crown for the Colts. Unfortunately, it also brought another first-round playoff loss, again to the Steelers, 40-14.

Jones and the Colts turned in yet a third stellar drive to the division crown in 1977, finishing 10-4. Their first-round playoff game was a Christmas Eve collision with Stabler and the Raiders, a double sudden-death overtime thriller. By any standards the game had a wild pace, but despite a superb performance by Jones and the Colts the Raiders were victorious, 36-31.

Although shoulder injuries brought an end to his career after a decade and he never got a shot at the Super Bowl, Jones' passing statistics rank him as one of the greatest in league history. He ranks fourteenth on the all-timer passer ratings list with a career rating of 78.2. In 10 seasons, he completed 1430 of 2551 attempts for 18,190 yards and 124 touchdowns.

Sonny Jurgensen

Christian A 'Sonny' Jurgensen's greatness was sandwiched between two career traffic jams. He joined the Philadelphia Eagles in 1957, only to find that he would have to wait for playing time while the legendary Norm Van Brocklin guided the team. Toward the close of his career, he found similar troubles on a Washington Redskins staff that included Billy Kilmer and Joe Theisman. Yet, in the years between the backups, Jurgensen found an open lane that took him all the way to the Hall of Fame.

He had been traded to Washington in 1964 and immediately became the chief Redskin. His targets were the likes of tight end Jerry Smith and running back Charley Taylor. Like their namesakes, the mid-1960s Redskins didn't win the big war, but earned their reputation ambushing the favorites, in particular Dandy Don Meredith and the Dallas Cowboys.

The first memorable matchup occurred on 28 November 1965, when Jurgy rallied the Skins from a 21-0 deficit, to a score of 31-20. Down 31-27 with less than two minutes to play, Jurgensen juggled timeouts and sideline patterns to give Washington the win, 34-31. The Cowboys got revenge the following 13 November, after Jurgensen pitched his way to a 30-28 Redskin lead late in the game. This time the golden two minutes were Meredith's, as he directed Dallas to the Skins' 12, where Danny Villaneuva punched up the winning kick, for a final score of 31-30.

A month later Washington met Dallas again, and with less than two minutes left and the score tied at 31-31, Jurgensen drove his team into scoring range, then bled the clock down, before Charley Gogolak kicked the winner, 34-31. Meredith evened things up the next October with another late drive – 71 yards in 43 seconds – to nip the Skins, 17-14.

Despite the burning arrows and gunsmoke, the Redskins fared pitifully in the league standings through the 1960s, until Vince Lombardi arrived as their coach in 1969 and inspired them to a 7-5-2 record. By the time George Allen arrived in 1971 to push Washington to the Super Bowl, Jurgensen's age and the constant battering he had taken over the years had caught up with him. Injured, he could only watch from the sidelines as Washington went to the Super Bowl with Billy Kilmer.

Regardless, his career passing statistics speak for themselves: 32,224 yards gained by completing 2433 of 4262 attempts and 255 touchdown passes. Jurgensen is rated seventh on the all-time list of NFL passers. He led the league four times in completions and five times in total yards. He retired in 1974 and was inducted into the Hall of Fame in 1983.

Opposite: *In 1976 Bert Jones had one of the best passing seasons in the history of the league, with a 102.6 rating.* **Above:** *Sonny Jurgensen holds his bronze bust at the 1983 Hall of Fame ceremonies.* **Right:** *Jurgensen passed for 32,224 yards and 255 TDs in his career.*

Joe Kapp

In his day, the sportswriters liked to speak of Minnesota Vikings quarterback Joe Kapp as a brawling, thuggish competitor, more suited to the bruising existence of an outside linebacker than to the finesse and headiness of a quarterback. There was a bit of truth in the depiction. But more than anything, Kapp was a throwback to the days when a quarterback barked signals and never hesitated to lower his head and buck the line for a few extra yards. Basically, Kapp did whatever was required to win.

An All-American at California in 1958, he was drafted eighteenth by the Washington Redskins in the 1959 draft. Rather than face those odds, Kapp took his skills to the Canadian Football League and played there eight seasons until the Vikings took him on as a free agent in 1967. Those who doubted his passing skills did a doubletake early in the 1969 season, when he bombed the defending NFL champions, the Baltimore Colts, for seven touchdowns in a 52-14 rout. His Vikings had lost the first game of the season to the New York Giants, 24-23, then reeled off 12 victories in a row before losing the last game of the regular season, 10-3, to the Atlanta Falcons. They nosed past the Los Angeles Rams in the first round of the playoffs to meet the Cleveland Browns for the NFL championship.

Kapp was masterful in the clutch. He rushed eight times for 57 yards, including a seven-yard touchdown run in the first quarter to open the scoring. On the day, he completed seven of 13 passing attempts for 169 yards, a performance marked by a 75-yard jewel in the first quarter to Gene Washington for a 14-0 lead. He drove the team to 13 more points before Minnesota allowed a single Cleveland touchdown.

With the 27-7 victory, the Vikings advanced to the Super Bowl opposite Len Dawson and the Kansas City Chiefs. The Vikings were favored, and although Kapp completed 16 of 25 passing attempts for 183 yards, he also threw two interceptions. Late in the second half, he injured his shoulder and left the game. With a perfect mix of defense and offense, the Chiefs won Super Bowl IV, 23-7. Kapp never took the Vikings back to the Super Bowl, but for an instant, a season, he had captured the crowd's imagination with his verve.

Jim Kelly

Because Jim Kelly had been a fine pro prospect in the cradle of quarterbacks, the University of Miami, the Buffalo Bills selected him in the first round of the 1983 NFL draft. But Kelly chose instead to accept the offer of the Houston Gamblers of the United States Football League.

There, he became the ultimate shootist in the Houston arsenal. In 1984, he passed for 5219 yards and 44 touchdowns over an 18-game season. The big numbers brought Kelly a good bit of attention, including a feature in *Sports Illustrated*, but many observers questioned if he would have done so well throwing against the talented secondaries of the NFL.

In 1986, the observers got their answer. Starting 16 games for the Bills, the 6-foot-3, 215-pounder completed 285 of 480 attempts for 3593 yards and 22 touchdowns against 17 interceptions for a solid 83.3 rating. Much of what Kelly accomplished as a passer was done without the benefit of a good offensive line.

Having accomplished one 5000 yard season, Kelly seems ready to challenge the passing records of the NFL in future seasons.

Opposite top: *Joe Kapp of the Minnesota Vikings celebrates after a 27-7 victory over Cleveland in the 1970 NFL championship.*
Opposite bottom: *Kapp displays his typical gutsy style as he leaps over a defender and into the end zone in the 1969 playoff against the Rams.*
Right: *The Buffalo Bills can hope for future success with quarterback Jim Kelly at the helm. The 6-foot 3-inch, 215-pound Kelly machine-gunned 22 touchdown passes in 1986.*

Jack Kemp

In 1960, American Football League executives knew that if their new franchises were going to make it in pro football, they would have to generate immediate excitement on the field. Fortunately, Jack Kemp was around to help them with their plan. The new league quickly established a reputation for gunslinging. In its first season, Kemp, who went on to fame as a conservative Congressman, became the first pro quarterback to break the 3000-yard mark in a season of passing. He totalled 3018 yards in leading the Los Angeles Chargers to the title game, where they lost to the Houston Oilers, 24-16.

For the 1961 season, Kemp again quarterbacked the Chargers, who had moved to San Diego, to the AFL championship game, where they lost again to the Oilers, 10-3. The 1963 season began as a shock for Kemp when the Chargers accidentally placed him on waivers because of an office error. He was quickly claimed by the Buffalo Bills. The Chargers replaced him with Tobin Rote, who teamed with Lance Alworth to take San Diego to the championship game. There, they bombed Boston and veteran quarterback Babe Parilli, 51-10.

The Chargers realized how much they regretted losing Kemp that next season, 1964, when he and the Bills defeated them in the championship game, 20-7. Kemp completed 10 of 20 passes for 168 yards and ran for a touchdown in taking his team to the title. In 1965

the Bills again met San Diego in the championship, and again won, 23-0. This time Kemp completed 9 of 20 passes for 152 yards and a touchdown. For 1966, he again drove the Bills to the AFL title game, only to see the Kansas City Chiefs defeat them, 31-7, thereby stealing the distinction of playing in Super Bowl I.

In six years, Kemp had done a job for the league, taking his teams to five division titles and two AFL championships. After football, Kemp moved into Republican politics and was elected to Congress.

52

Bill Kenney

Opposite top: *Jack Kemp of the Buffalo Bills steps into the pocket. He carried Buffalo to the AFL championship game in 1966.*
Opposite bottom: *Kemp, now a US Congressman, passed for over 3000 yards in 1960.*
Right: *In just eight NFL seasons, Bill Kenney of the Kansas City Chiefs has completed 1118 out of 2043 passing attempts and thrown for 14,621 yards and 90 TDs.*

Bill Kenney made the roster of the Kansas City Chiefs as a free agent out of Northern Colorado in 1979. Although he has played for a struggling franchise, Kenney has survived to become one of the highest rated passers in the history of the league.

After eight seasons in the NFL, Kenney ranks seventeenth on the league's all-time career passing charts with a 77.5 rating, just behind Frank Ryan and Johnny Unitas. Going into the 1987 season, Kenney had completed 1118 of 2043 attempts for 14,621 yards and 90 touchdown passes.

In 1983, he had seven games in which he threw for more than 300 yards, including four consecutive 300-yard games. That December against San Diego, he completed 31 of 41 passes for 411 yards and four touchdowns.

In 1986, the Chiefs used strong defense and special teams to reach the playoffs for the first time in 16 years. In a crucial late-season game against the Los Angeles Raiders, Kenney threw a 26-yard scoring pass to Stephone Paige in the fourth quarter to give the Chiefs a 20-17 win.

Billy Kilmer

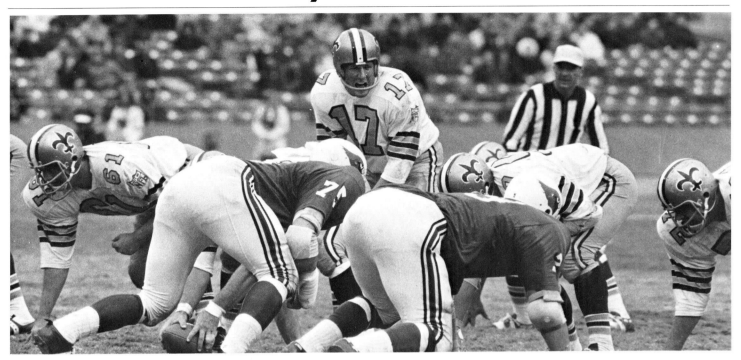

Billy Kilmer was an All-American at UCLA and a first-round draft pick of the San Francisco 49ers in 1961. San Francisco used him as a backup to John Brodie until the NFL expanded in the early 1970s. Then Kilmer was taken in the draft by the New Orleans Saints.

Fortunately for Kilmer, Washington Redskins coach George Allen talked New Orleans into trading him. In Washington, Kilmer joined Sonny Jurgensen and Joe Theismann in vying for the starting role as leader of Allen's 'Over The Hill Gang,' the group of aging players assembled to give the Redskins an instantly competitive team in 1972. Jurgensen, however, was hurt, and Theismann was still an apprentice.So Kilmer, in the twelfth season of his career, finally got the opportunity to show the football world what he could

do. For the year, he completed 120 of 225 attempts for 1648 yards and 19 touchdowns. But beyond his passing, he brought a toughness to the Redskins. On the strength of that, they ground out an 11-3 record and conquered their perennial foes, the Dallas Cowboys, for the division crown.

The victory sent the Redskins into Super Bowl VII against the undefeated Miami Dolphins. The joy ride stopped for Kilmer and the Over The Hill Gang in Los Angeles' Memorial Coliseum. The Miami defense stopped the heralded Redskins running game, forcing Kilmer to pass more than he liked. He completed 14 of 28 attempts for 104 yards but threw three interceptions. Miami won, 14-7. But during that golden season Kilmer had made his point.

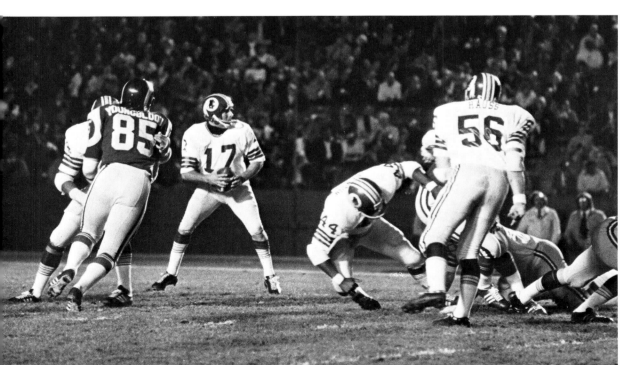

Above: *Billy Kilmer played briefly for the New Orleans Saints in the early 1970s.*
Left: *Kilmer has plenty of time and protection as he gets set to fire one of his three TD passes for the Redskins in a 23-17 win over Los Angeles on 9 December 1974.*
Opposite top: *Not even a flying linebacker can distract young Bernie Kosar of the Cleveland Browns as he prepares to launch a pass in a 24-21 win over Detroit on 28 September 1986.*

Bernie Kosar

Bernie Kosar set a covey of passing records at the University of Miami and led the Hurricanes to the 1984 National Championship. Then with two years of college eligibility remaining, he graduated ahead of his class and joined the AFL's Cleveland Browns.

In only his second season, 1986, Kosar passed for 3854 yards and led his team to its best finish in half a decade. A crucial late-season game against Pittsburgh went to overtime tied at 31, until Kosar ended it with an off-balance 36-yard touchdown pass to receiver Webster Slaughter. Three weeks later, he and the Browns went into Cincinnati's Riverfront Stadium for a showdown with the Bengals over the AFC's Central Division crown. On the first play of the game, Kosar lofted a 66-yard bomb to receiver Reggie Langhorne, shoving the Browns off on their way to a 34-3 rout and the title.

Against San Diego in the last game of the season, he completed 21 of 28 attempts for 258 yards and two touchdowns as Cleveland won, 47-17, and finished the regular season 12-4, the most wins in a season for a Browns team since they joined the NFL in 1950. But in the AFC divisional playoffs against the New York Jets, Kosar struggled. He threw two interceptions and found his team down 20-10 with a little over four minutes remaining. That's when he showed he was a miracle worker.

First, he drove the Browns 68 yards to set up Kevin Mack's one-yard scoring run with 1:57 left. After New York punted, Kosar set the Browns sailing down the field. A 37-yard pass to Slaughter put Cleveland at New York's five, where kicker Mark Moseley tied the game with seven seconds left. In the first overtime, Kosar drove the team to field goal range, but Moseley missed. In the second overtime, Kosar again moved the Browns into field goal range. After 17:02 of extra play, Moseley kicked a 27-yarder for a 23-20 win. Kosar set NFL postseason records for passing attempts (64), yardage (489) and average gain per attempt (14.81 yards). He tied another by completing 33 passes.

The next week, he took his team to the verge of the Super Bowl, by rallying the Browns for 10 fourth-quarter points, including a 48-yard scoring pass to Brian Brennan for a 20-13 lead. Then Kosar had to watch as Denver quarterback John Elway pulled a similar trick, driving the Broncos 98 yards to tie the game at 20. In overtime, the Browns stumbled and the Broncos prevailed by a field goal, 23-20. Still, the Cleveland fans stood for a prolonged ovation afterward. They knew they had a quarterback for the future.

Tommy Kramer

A first-round draft pick out of Rice University in 1977, Tommy Kramer was the Minnesota Vikings' choice to take over for retiring veteran Fran Tarkenton. Kramer led the Vikings to a 9-7 record and the NFC's Central Division crown in 1980, but then the team struggled through a series of coaching changes and hangdog seasons. Kramer stuck with his team but was unable to reverse the downward trend.

Finally, in 1986, the Vikings got back on track as Kramer won the NFC passing crown with a 92.6 rating. On the season, he completed 208 of 372 attempts for 3000 yards and 24 touchdowns against only 10 interceptions, enough to drive Minnesota to a 9-7 record. They finished just out of the running for the playoffs, but Kramer received a deserved invitation to the Pro Bowl.

Dave Krieg

Out of little Milton College, Dave Krieg made the roster of the Seattle Seahawks as a free agent in 1980. Over the next seven seasons, the 6-foot-1, 197-pounder has racked up the statistics to make him the fourth-highest rated career passer in NFL history. In seven years, he has completed 1046 of 1822 attempts for 107 touchdowns and 13,677 yards against 73 interceptions. His 84.1 career passing rating ranks him behind only Dan Marino, Joe Montana and Otto Graham.

In 1983, Krieg led the Seahawks to the AFC championship game only to turn in a rare miserable performance. He completed only three of nine attempts with three interceptions before being replaced by Jim Zorn. The Seahawks lost to the Raiders, 30-14.

Over four seasons, 1983-86, Krieg has thrown 98

Opposite: *Tommy Kramer of the Minnesota Vikings turned in a stellar performance in the 1986 season, taking the NFC passing title and playing in the Pro Bowl.*

Above left: *Seattle Seahawk Dave Krieg blitzes a bullet in a game against the Miami Dolphins.*
Above: *Krieg ranks fourth in the NFL's career passing list.*

touchdown passes, a mark bettered only by Dan Marino of the Dolphins. For 1986, Krieg was the third-highest rated passer in the NFL with a 91.0 performance. He led the Seahawks to a 10-6 record but played poorly at midseason, contributing to four losses that kept them out of the playoffs.

Regardless, Krieg has proven himself a heady quarterback whose performance over seven years ranks him among the game's best passers.

Daryle Lamonica

For much of the 1960s Daryle Lamonica and the Oakland Raiders lorded over the American Football League. Twice Lamonica led the AFL in passing. In 1967, he completed 220 of 425 attempts for 3228 yards and 30 touchdowns. In 1970, the numbers were 179 of 356 for 2516 yards and 22 TDs.

But Lamonica, a Notre Dame product, was best known for driving the Raiders to the league championship game, a feat he accomplished for four consecutive seasons, 1967-70. As a result, he holds several records as one of pro football's all-time 'playoff quarterbacks.' Against Houston in the 1969 playoffs, he threw six touchdown passes, an NFL record. In all, Lamonica threw 19 touchdown passes in 13 playoff games.

In 1963, he broke in with the Buffalo Bills, where he set a playoff record for the longest completion by throwing a 93-yard TD pass versus Boston. But most of Lamonica's reputation was earned as a Raider. For the 1967 season, he threw a whopping 425 times, leading to his nickname 'The Mad Bomber.' With Lamonica at the controls, the Raiders offense scored 468 points and finished the regular schedule 13-1.

Yet in the AFL championship game against Houston, Lamonica suddenly turned down the passing frequency as the Raiders found a new winning formula. He completed only 10 of 24 attempts for 111 yards and two touchdowns, but he also ran for a third score as the Raiders humbled the Houston Oilers, 40-7, to earn a spot opposite the Green Bay Packers in Super Bowl II. Against pro football's best defense, Lamonica completed 15 of 34 for 208 yards and two touchdowns, but it wasn't nearly enough. Showing one of the strongest teams in the history of the game, the Packers took their second title, 33-14.

The next year, Lamonica battled the New York Jets' Joe Namath to give the AFL its most exciting championship game ever. Lamonica had a Mad Bomber day, completing 20 of 47 for 401 yards and a TD, but Namath and the Jets squeezed by, 27-23. A year later, the AFL held its final championship game, and Lamonica again made sure his Raiders were one of the participants. Oakland had beaten the Kansas City Chiefs twice during the regular season, but the Chiefs forced Lamonica into throwing three interceptions and won, 17-7. For a fourth straight year, Lamonica took his team to the title game in 1970. But he was injured in the first half and was replaced by veteran George Blanda, who fell victim to interceptions late in the game. The Baltimore Colts prevailed, 27-17.

Lamonica would later hand the Oakland reins over to a young Ken Stabler, but the team's management knew that in his day 'The Mad Bomber' had lifted the franchise to a new level of competition.

Greg Landry

The Detroit Lions selected All-American quarterback Greg Landry from the University of Massachusetts in the first round of the 1968 draft, beginning a 17-year pro career that included 11 years with the Lions, followed by stints with the Baltimore Colts and Chicago Bears of the NFL, and two United States Football League teams.

As an NFL quarterback, Landry completed 1276 of 2300 attempts for 16,502 yards and 98 touchdowns. He also rushed for 2654 yards (a 6.2 average) and scored 20 touchdowns. He helped lead Detroit to a wild card spot in the playoffs with a 10-4 record in 1970. Landry was named to the Pro Bowl in 1972 and put his name in the Pro Bowl record books by throwing 11 passes for 122 yards, an average gain of 11.09 yards.

Landry also had the dubious distinction of being sacked 11 times in a game against Dallas in 1975.

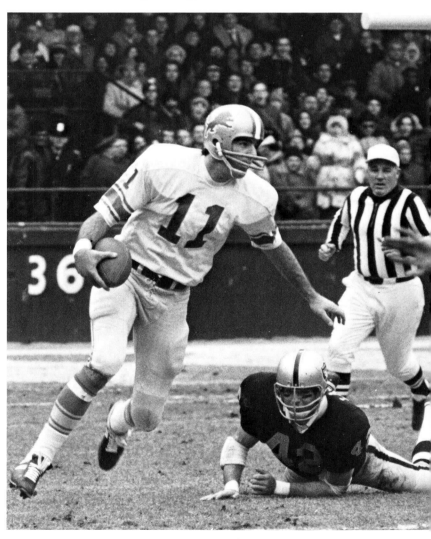

Left: *Oakland Raider Daryle Lamonica has to chuckle as he easily slides through the Kansas City Chiefs defense for a four-yard touchdown run.*

Above: *Greg Landry of the Detroit Lions rolls around the end for a big 16-yard gain against the Oakland Raiders on 26 November 1970.*

Bobby Layne

Bobby Layne had been a talented tailback at the University of Texas in the 1940s. He was a first-round draft pick of the Chicago Bears in 1948. The pros, it seemed, were eager to fashion Layne into a T-formation quarterback.

Yet it wasn't until 1952 that the freewheeling Layne began to realize his potential. A 6-foot-2, 190-pounder, Layne had done a stint with the New York Bulldogs of the All American Football Conference in 1949 before moving to the Lions in 1950.

With the Lions, Layne rejoined his high-school teammate, Doak Walker, who had played his college ball at Southern Methodist. Together, they gave Detroit one of the most talented backfields in the league. Teamed with another Texas boy, defensive back Yale Lary, they powered the Lions to the 1952 NFL championship over the Cleveland Browns, 17-7.

Still, the experts noted that the Browns had mostly fumbled the game away, and the Lions seemed to have something to prove all over again when they met the Browns for the 1953 championship. All in all, the 1953 game was marked by tremendous defense. But as always seems the case, the golden moments fell to the quarterbacks and receivers, and like any great NFL quarterback, Layne was eager for the gold.

In the first half, the Lions sacked and befuddled the normally unshakeable Browns quarterback Otto Graham into connecting on only 2 of 15 attempts for 31 yards. While he struggled, Detroit forged ahead, as Walker added a field goal, giving Detroit a 10-3 halftime lead. The Cleveland players were steamed in a scathing talk from coach Paul Brown at intermission, which was enough to reverse the tide in the third quarter. Layne contributed two turnovers to the Browns' effort. First, he threw an interception, which led to Cleveland's drive to tie the score. Then at the end of the quarter, Layne fumbled, the Browns recovered and Lou Groza kicked a field goal for a 13-10 lead. With 4:10 to play, Groza added another field goal for a 16-10 lead that seemed solid on a day dominated by defense.

It was the type of challenge Layne thrived on.

Detroit's last-ditch drive concluded with a 33-yard touchdown pass to end Jim Doran, just one of the many completions that nailed down Layne's reputation as the original comeback quarterback. It also helped reserve him a place in the Hall of Fame. The home crowd roared that day as Walker came on the field to kick the extra point, for a 17-16 Detroit championship.

The Browns salved any hurt they might have felt the next year, just as the football world was thinking Layne and the Lions had a dynasty. The teams met for a third consecutive championship bout, but Cleveland whipped the favored Lions, 56-10, for the 1954 championship. Layne suffered through a terrible day, throwing six interceptions.

Layne again helped the Lions to the championship round in 1957, but he was injured and couldn't play the last two games of the season. Regardless, his championship spirit was obvious. He was traded to the Pittsburgh Steelers for the 1958 season and immediately helped the perennial doormats become winners. He retired from professional football after the 1962 season.

Layne was inducted into the Hall of Fame in 1967. He died 1 December 1986, three weeks before his sixtieth birthday.

Opposite: *Bobby Layne (22), drafted by the Chicago Bears in the first round in 1948, is shown here with former Bear greats Johnny Lujack (left) and Sid Luckman (middle).*
Above left: *Bobby Layne's legendary comebacks and competitive savvy landed him a spot in the Hall of Fame in 1967.*
Above right: *Layne threw the winning touchdown pass to Jim Doran in the 1953 championship game to claim a 17-16 Detroit win over the Cleveland Browns.*
Right: *Layne moves to his right to hand off to a running back.*

Eddie LeBaron

Left: *Eddie LeBaron, when he played for the Dallas Cowboys in 1962. Drafted by Washington in 1950, LeBaron chalked up Redskins player of the year honors in 1955 and 1958, as well going to the Pro Bowl for three years (1956, 1957 and 1959).*
Opposite: *Neil Lomax of the St Louis Cardinals goes down begrudgingly in a game against the Green Bay Packers in 1983.*

Eddie LeBaron was only 5-foot-7, but he managed to make his mark as a pro quarterback despite spending his career carrying weak teams with his talent.

An All-American at the University of the Pacific, LeBaron was drafted by the Washington Redskins in 1950 but entered the Marines for two years, where he led the Quantico base team against a schedule of major colleges. He left the service in 1952 and signed again with the Redskins.

Washington, a once-proud franchise, had fallen on losing times. From a 4-8 finish in 1952, LeBaron gave the Skins their first winning season in several years in 1953, when he drove the offense to a 6-5-1 record. In 1955, Washington finished 8-4 and second place in the Eastern Conference as LeBaron threw for 1270 yards and nine touchdowns. As much as for his arm, LeBaron was valued for his ballhandling skills. His profession recognized his ability by naming him to the Pro

Bowl in 1956, 1957 and 1959. In 1958, LeBaron led the NFL in passing, completing 79 of 145 attempts for 1365 yards and 11 touchdowns.

Twice – in 1955 and 1958 – LeBaron was named the Redskins player of the year, but in 1960, the team traded him to the new NFL franchise, the Dallas Cowboys, where he served as Tom Landry's starting quarterback for three seasons. The Cowboys improved each year under the aging LeBaron, while the Cowboys' young superstar, Don Meredith, matured as his backup. In 1962, LeBaron's final season as a starter for Dallas, he completed 95 of 166 passes for 1436 yards and 16 touchdowns against nine interceptions for a 95.3 rating, the third highest in the league that year.

Over the course of his ten-year pro football career, LeBaron passed for a total of more than 11,000 yards and 90 touchdowns.

Neil Lomax

In six years as a pro quarterback, Neil Lomax of the St Louis Cardinals has rung up statistics that rank him among the greatest passers in the history of the game. He has achieved his ranking despite playing for an uncertain team in St Louis.

Drafted in the second round out of Portland State in 1981, Lomax helped reverse the Cardinals' fortunes and led the team to winning seasons in 1982, 1983 and 1984. In 1984, Lomax set a Cardinals club record by passing for 4614 yards and 28 touchdowns, which led to predictions of greatness for 1985. The team, however, had a disastrous 5-11 year, despite Lomax's solid passing statistics (265 of 471 for 3214 yards, 18 touchdowns, 12 interceptions and a 79.5 rating).

If St Louis has a bright spot in its football future, it is Neil Lomax. In six seasons, he has completed 1287 of 2247 attempts for 15,959 yards and 92 touchdowns against 67 interceptions for an 80.7 career rating, enough to rank Lomax eleventh in the NFL's all-time career ratings.

Sid Luckman

With their T-formation, man-in-motion offense, the Chicago Bears dominated the NFL during World War II, powering their way to five title game appearances and four championships from 1940 to 1946. The superior athlete at the core of that dynasty was quarterback Sid Luckman.

The average passing gain of the Bears in the 1940s still ranks higher in the record books than most of the high-tech offenses of today. Luckman led the league in passing yards in 1943, 1945 and 1946, but he did much more for his team than throw the ball.

An Ivy Leaguer, Luckman came to the NFL from Columbia in 1939. As a second-year pro, he led the Bears to their astounding 73-0 upset of the Washington Redskins in the 1940 NFL championship. With Luckman's strong arm running the offense the next season, the Bears racked up a record 396 points in 1941 against an 11-game schedule. They beat Green Bay in a playoff game (the league had adopted the use of playoff games earlier that year) and faced New York in the league title game at Wrigley Field. Tougher than expected, the Giants trailed only 9-6 at the half, but the Bears erupted for four second-half touchdowns (Norm Standlee, the 230-pound rookie out of Stanford scored twice) to win their second consecutive championship, 38-9.

Bears coach George Halas entered the service after the 1941 season, but Chicago was still favored to win a

Above: *Sid Luckman of the Chicago Bears.*
Below: *Luckman (left center) and coach George Halas (right center).*

Opposite top: *Luckman wings one downfield.*
Opposite bottom: *Johnny Lujack (left) and Sid Luckman.*

third consecutive title in 1942. Coached by Hunk Anderson and Luke Johnson, the Bears finished the regular season 11-0, but were upset in the title game by the Redskins, 14-6.

Luckman answered that disappointment with what was considered his greatest season in 1943. He turned in the NFL's first 400-yard passing game when he hit 21 of 32 for 433 yards and a record seven touchdowns against the New York Giants on 14 November 1943 at the Polo Grounds. The game had been billed as 'Sid Luckman Day' to honor the Brooklyn boy who had gone to greatness with the Bears. In the emotion of that setting, Luckman responded with the greatest performance by a quarterback to that date. His seven touchdown passes have since been equalled but never bettered.

Again in 1943, Luckman guided his team to the NFL title game, and again the opponent was Washington. But this time Luckman took control. He closed out a fantastic season by throwing five touchdown passes to destroy the Redskins, 41-21.

After the 1943 season, Luckman joined the Merchant Marines (638 NFL players entered the service during World War II), and the Bears got a look at their future without him. They were nosed out of the cham-

pionship game by the Packers. But after the war, Luckman and Halas both returned to the Bears and took them to another NFL title in 1946, this time over the New York Giants, 24-14.

Luckman remained in the league with Chicago until 1950, when he retired. Although the Bears never returned to the title game in the 1940s, they never fell below second place in the Western Division. Luckman was inducted into the Hall of Fame in 1965.

Johnny Lujack

Johnny Lujack came out of the service after World War II to lead Notre Dame to undefeated seasons in 1946 and 1947. For that performance, he won the Heisman trophy in 1947, beating out other distinguished college quarterbacks such as Charlie Conerly at Mississippi, Harry Gilmer at Alabama and Bobby Layne at Texas. Lujack had played his first game for Notre Dame in 1943. Against Army in that debut, he threw for two touchdowns, ran for another and intercepted a pass as the Irish won, 26-0.

He joined the Chicago Bears for the 1948 season, and as a rookie in the age of two-way players, he intercepted eight passes. In 1949, he became only the fourth player in the history of pro football to pass for more than 400 yards, when he completed 24 of 39 for 468 yards and six touchdowns against the Chicago Cardinals, the team that had gone to the NFL championship game the year before. His 468 yards was a new single-game record at the time.

He led the Bears in scoring for four years and was named to the Pro Bowl in 1950 and 1951, his last years in the league. In the four years he quarterbacked the Bears, they compiled a 35-13 record. In 1950, he pushed the team to the conference championship, only to see Chicago fall 24-14 to the Los Angeles Rams.

Upon his retirement as a player, he returned to Notre Dame as a backfield coach. He was elected to the National Football Foundation Hall of Fame in 1960.

Archie Manning

Left: *New Orleans Saints quarterback Archie Manning leaves Chicago Bear pursuers behind as he races for a touchdown in 1977.*
Above: *Manning turns upfield against the Rams. A Pro Bowler in 1980, he passed for 3716 yards and 23 touchdowns that season.*

Quarterback Archie Manning led a resurgence in football at the University of Mississippi in the early 1970s. In the 1970 Sugar Bowl, he led Ole Miss to a 27-22 win over Arkansas by throwing for 273 yards and two touchdowns.

The next year, he took the Rebs to the Gator Bowl, despite having to play with a broken arm protected by a plastic sleeve. He shrugged off the injury and rushed for 95 yards and passed for 180. He finished fourth in the 1969 Heisman trophy voting and third in 1970 behind Pat Sullivan and Joe Theismann.

A gritty, gutsy performer in college, Manning took those same qualities to his pro career with the New Orleans Saints, where he labored for a decade trying to make a bad team better. From 1971 to 1982, Manning passed for 21,734 yards and 115 touchdowns, all club records. His best statistical season was 1980, when he threw for 3716 and 23 touchdowns, also club records. Manning was named to the Pro Bowl in 1980, where he helped the NFC to victory and set a Pro Bowl record by completing nine of 10 passes for a 90 percent completion rate. He finished his career with the Minnesota Vikings in 1984.

Dan Marino

At age 25, after only four seasons in the NFL, Miami Dolphins quarterback Dan Marino had amassed enough records and statistics to convince many observers that he is one of the greatest quarterbacks ever to play the game. The final analysis on that issue will probably come down to the number of championships his teams win.

His first season, 1983, Marino set records for the highest rating (96.0) for a rookie passer in the history of the league and for the lowest percentage of interceptions for a rookie (2.03). In 1984, he drilled Miami to a 14-2 record and 514 total points. In doing that, he became the first pro passer to break the 5000-yard barrier in a season (5084 net gained), and he set league records for touchdown passes (48) and passes completed (362).

He has led the league in completions, yards gained and touchdown passes for three consecutive seasons, 1984-86. In seven games he has thrown for more than 400 yards and in nine others for more than 300. In 12 games, he has thrown four touchdown passes or more. In 1986, he threw 44 touchdown passes and broke his own record for completions with 378. Those statistics give him the highest career rating as a passer in the history of the league (95.2). In four years, he has completed 1248 of 2050 attempts for 16,177 yards and 142 touchdowns against only 67 interceptions.

In the AFC championship game in 1984, Marino completed 21 of 32 attempts for 421 yards and four touchdowns. He also threw an interception, but his performance blasted Miami past Pittsburgh, 45-28. But in the Super Bowl, his 318 yards passing (completed 29 of 50) was blemished by two interceptions, as San Francisco won, 38-16. The next season, he

again drove Miami to the AFC title game, this time against New England. But Marino had another off day, completing only 20 of 48 for 248 yards and two interceptions, as the Patriots won, 31-14.

Certainly Dan Marino seems headed for the Hall of Fame. Still, he's made it known on more than one occasion that passing numbers are nice, but a Super Bowl championship is what he wants most.

Bernie Masterson

Bernie Masterson came to the Chicago Bears out of Nebraska in 1934, and for the next seven years his quarterbacking was an important element in the team's offense.

In the 1930s, when passing was in its early developmental stages, Masterson completed a whopping 8.3 percent of his attempts for touchdowns. In 1937, he led the Bears to the Western Divison crown and the NFL championship game, where his two touchdown passes gave Chicago a 21-14 lead over the Washington Redskins heading into the fourth quarter. But the performance of Redskins rookie sensation Sammy Baugh propelled Washington to a 28-21 win.

For two seasons, 1937 and 1938, Masterson led the league in the highest average gain from his passes. In seven seasons with the Bears, Masterson threw for 3366 yards and 34 touchdowns.

Below: *Bernie Masterson holds for placekicker Jack Manders. The Chicago quarterback took the Bears to the 1937 NFL championship.*

Opposite left: *Barring injury, Dan Marino of the Miami Dolphins just might break every NFL passing record ever set.*
Above: *Marino waits for the right moment to release his pass.*

Above: *Defiant Chicago Bears quarterback Jim McMahon sports his infamous Rozelle headband.*
Right: *McMahon led his team to a dominating season and a Super Bowl victory in 1985.*
Opposite bottom: *'Dandy Don' Meredith (17) of the Dallas Cowboys consults coach Tom Landry and Eddie LeBaron (14) during a game against Philadelphia on 17 November 1963.*

Jim McMahon

It is perhaps surprising that the 1980s had produced only one truly great loud-mouthed signal caller, just one throwback to the legacy of Joe Namath: the Chicago Bears' Jim McMahon.

A star at Brigham Young, McMahon came into the league in 1982 as a first-round draft choice armed with the confidence that he had set 71 college records for passing and total offense. His passing efficiency rating in college was the highest ever at 156.9, bettering the record set by Danny White at Arizona State, 148.9.

He continued that pace as a rookie with the Bears, completing 181 of 269 passes, a 57.14 percentage, the second highest for a rookie in the history of the league. That performance was enough to earn him the UPI NFC Rookie of the Year award.

By 1984, he had helped quarterback the Bears to the Central Division crown. But a series of injuries – a fractured hand, a bruised back, a lacerated kidney – required that he miss seven games as well as the playoffs. His career became a struggle to show flashes of brilliance between injuries. As a starter, he pushed the Bears to a 37-12 record. He fought off shoulder injuries in 1985 to lead Chicago to the Super Bowl, where he played with abandon, rushing for two touchdowns and completing 12 of 20 for 256 yards as his team won, 46-10.

A team player, McMahon has placed his advancement as a passer second to the needs of the Bears, a squad featuring a dominant defense and strong running game. As a result, McMahon doesn't carry the passing reputation he enjoyed in college. His career high as a pro passer (298 yards) came against Green Bay in 1983. Yet when the Bears need his offensive punch, he has often produced it instantly. Out of the lineup because of injuries, he entered a game against the Vikings in 1985 with Chicago trailing 17-9. In a little more than a quarter, he threw two touchdown passes and spurred the Bears to a 33-24 win.

He required shoulder surgery after being injured in 1986, and headed into the 1987 season with his playing status in doubt. Facing the prospect of having his career cut short, McMahon still has the consolation that he accomplished more in five years than many pro quarterbacks do in a decade.

Don Meredith

Don Meredith, a consensus All-American at Southern Methodist University, finished third in the 1959 Heisman trophy voting, and was selected in the first round of the pro draft by the Dallas Cowboys, a new team in the NFL, and the Dallas Texans of the brand new AFL.

Meredith chose the Cowboys and almost immediately began establishing his reputation as 'Dandy Don,' late-night partier and hard-living character. In those first years in the league, he served as an understudy to the veteran Eddie LeBaron. Yet Meredith's career and the success of the young franchise seemed to blossom simultaneously.

By 1966, he had driven Dallas to the NFL's Eastern Conference championship with a 10-3-1 record. Over the next two years, Meredith and the Cowboys would challenge one of the greatest teams in pro football, the Green Bay Packers of Vince Lombardi.

In the 1966 championship game, played at the Cotton Bowl in Dallas, Meredith and the Cowboys fought the Packers nose-to-nose into the third quarter, when the score stood 21-20, Green Bay. Then the Packers scored two touchdowns for what appeared a safe lead, 34-20. Meredith shook their faith with a 68-yard touchdown pass to tight end Frank Clarke. Then the dandy quarterback drove his team right into the face of foot-ball's best defense, down to the Green Bay one yard line, where with time running out, the Cowboys were called offsides. Instead of tying the game and sending the championship into overtime, the Cowboys struggled from the Packer 5 and lost, 34-27. Yet Meredith had completed 15 of 31 passes for 238 yards (he also threw an interception) against the legendary Packers secondary.

The next year he repeated the trick, driving Dallas to the Capitol Division title with a 9-5 record, then supervising a 52-14 demolition of Cleveland in the playoffs. Once again, Meredith and the Cowboys met the Packers in the championship game, and once again the result was an NFL legend. The game is known as the Ice Bowl, because it was played on frozen Lambeau Field in Milwaukee. The Packers jumped to a 14-0 lead, and Meredith calmly brought the Cowboys back through the cold, giving them a 17-14 fourth-quarter lead with a 50-yard touchdown pass to Lance Rentzel. Then all Meredith could do was watch as the Packers drove the length of the field in the final minutes to score on a dive as time ran down. The Packers had prevailed again, 21-17.

Out of patience with the chorus of Monday morning quarterbacks, Meredith retired soon afterward.

Joe Montana

The San Francisco 49ers were the surprise of the NFC in 1981. Finishing 2-14 in 1979, they surged to 13-3 over the 1981 regular season. The backbone of the team was an unsung defense, but the star of the show was quarterback Joe Montana. Since his college days at Notre Dame, he had shown a knack for coming back.

Montana's big moment came against the Dallas Cowboys in the NFC championship game played at Candlestick Park on 10 January 1982. Although trivia buffs will recall he threw three interceptions that day, the moment of truth came at the Dallas six on third and three with 58 seconds left. The 49ers trailed, 27-21. Montana was to look for Freddie Solomon in the left of the end zone, but the primary receiver was covered,

and the Dallas rush, led by 6-foot-9 Ed 'Too Tall' Jones, was bearing down. So Montana exited to his right, bought just enough time, and lofted a high one, just as the Dallas boys crashed in. Dwight Clark, 6-foot-4, waiting at the back of the end zone, leaped up and grabbed the ball. Ray Wersching's conversion put the 49ers in the Super Bowl, 28-27.

At the Super Bowl versus the Cincinnati Bengals, the San Francisco defense took center stage although Montana, Clark and Solomon did their part. From the momentum of a tremendous goal-line stand, San Francisco went on to win its first Super Bowl, 26-21. For the game, Montana had completed 14 of 22 pass attempts for 157 yards and a touchdown. He was named the game's Most Valuable Player, prompting coach Bill Walsh to tell reporters, 'Montana will be the great quarterback of the future. He is one of the coolest competitors of all time and he has just started.'

As Walsh predicted, Montana brought his team back to the Super Bowl in 1984. But the 'great quarterback of the future' laurels that season had gone to Miami's Dan Marino, who was having a record-breaking season. Montana and the 49ers, meanwhile, had set a record of their own, for regular-season wins' by going 15-1. The Dolphins zipped by Seattle and Pittsburgh in the preliminaries, running up 76 points in two games. The 49ers, meanwhile, knocked off two developing teams, the Chicago Bears and New York Giants, to make the meeting of Super Bowl XIX at Stanford Stadium.

Unfortunately for the Dolphins, Montana and the rest of the San Francisco team had tired of hearing how great Miami was in the pre-game hype. With three second-quarter touchdowns, the 49ers sealed the Dolphins' tomb and went on to bury them, 38-16. A profoundly disappointed Marino had thrown for 318 yards but also had two crucial interceptions. Montana, ever the Golden Boy, completed 24 of 35 attempts for a Super Bowl record 331 yards and three touchdowns, enough for everybody's MVP award.

Two seasons later, in 1986, Montana showed the sports world his grit was even greater than his flash. He was sidelined by a back injury that doctors feared would end his career. Yet Montana came back miraculously just weeks after surgery and guided the 49ers into the playoffs. Unfortunately the New York Giants, on their way to a world championship, humiliated San Francisco, 49-3, and put Montana out of the game.

Nevertheless, Montana's fans don't doubt that the master of comebacks will find a way back to the top. His place in the Hall of Fame seems secure. In the eight seasons from 1979 to 1986, he passed for 21,498 yards and 141 touchdowns. He ranks second on the all-time passer list – right behind Marino. And all 49ers fans know how Montana does in head-to-head competition with Miami's Dandy Dan.

Warren Moon

Warren Moon played his college ball at the University of Washington, then took his game farther north to play in the Canadian Football League for the Edmonton Eskimoes.

In six seasons in Canada, Moon built a reputation as one of the game's prolific passers. In each of his last two seasons in Canada, he passed for more than 5000 yards. In 1983, he completed 380 of 664 attempts for 5648 yards over 18 games.

In 1984, he joined the Houston Oilers as a free agent and set NFL records for the most yards passing by a rookie (3338) and most completions by a rookie (259). His completion percentage (57.66) was the third highest in the history of the league for a rookie. He passed for 2709 yards in 1985 and 3489 in 1986.

Opposite: *Montana hands off to running back Wendell Tyler. One of today's most promising young quarterbacks, Montana seems destined to be a record-breaker and a candidate for the Hall of Fame.*

Right: *Formerly a star in the Canadian League, Warren Moon moved to Houston in 1984, where during a fabulous season he set records for yards passing and completions by a rookie.*

Earl Morrall

In 1956, the San Francisco 49ers selected Michigan State quarterback Earl Morrall in the first round of the NFL draft. From there, Morrall travelled around the league, playing with Pittsburgh, Detroit and the New York Giants. In 1968, he came to the Baltimore Colts as a backup to Johnny Unitas.

In the last preseason game, Unitas tore his right elbow, and at age 34, Morrall moved to the forefront. For the season, he completed 182 of 317 attempts for 2909 yards and 26 touchdowns against only 17 interceptions, good enough to earn the NFL passing crown. Even better, Morrall's performance propelled the Colts to 402 points and a 13-1 record. In the playoffs, he engineered a 24-14 pasting of Minnesota, then guided the Colts in one of the most decisive NFL championship wins ever, a 34-0 massacre of the powerful Cleveland Browns. The win made the Colts heavy favorites in Super Bowl III against Joe Namath and the New York Jets. Unfortunately, Namath threw for 206 yards and Morrall had three interceptions as

the Jets pulled off one of football's greatest upsets, 16-7.

For 1972, Morrall again came to the rescue, this time for the Miami Dolphins. Regular Dolphins quarterback Bob Griese was injured in the fifth game, and Morrall came on to lead Miami to nine straight wins for an unbeaten regular season. In the process, he won the AFC passing crown by completing 83 of 150 attempts for 1360 yards and 11 touchdowns against seven interceptions.

He quarterbacked the Dolphins to a 20-14 win over the Cleveland Browns in the first round of the playoffs. In the second round, Griese returned to action and took Miami to the Super Bowl and an undefeated season. As was his style, the 38-year-old Morrall stepped gracefully into the background. He said he would have liked to have started in the Super Bowl against the Washington Redskins, but he declined to question Coach Don Shula's decision publicly. Regardless, Morrall had been granted his moments in the spotlight and played them to the fullest.

Craig Morton

Craig Morton had the grit of a competitor, fierce enough to face 18 seasons of pass rush in the NFL. During that time, he quarterbacked teams to the AFC championship and the NFL championship. Morton ranks seventeenth on the all-time list for passes attempted (3786), sixteenth on the list for passes completed (2053), twentieth in touchdown passes (183), and sixteenth in total passing yardage (27,908).

The Dallas Cowboys selected 6-foot-4, 215-pound Morton out of the University of California in the first round of the 1965 draft. He took over the passing chores in Tom Landry's sophisticated offense when Don Meredith retired after the 1968 season.

For the 1969 season, he led Dallas to a 11-2-1 record and the Capitol Division crown by completing 162 of 302 attempts for 2619 yards and 21 touchdowns against 15 interceptions. The Cowboys lost to the Cleveland Browns in the playoffs, 38-14. But Morton brought them back again the next year. For 1970, they again claimed the Capitol Division with a 10-4 record, as he completed 102 of 207 passes for 1819 yards and 15 touchdowns. With only seven interceptions, he finished the season with a solid 89.7 pass rating. And the Cowboys finished their season in the Super Bowl. Morton directed them past Detroit and San Francisco in the playoffs, but couldn't quite get them past Baltimore in Super Bowl V. He threw three interceptions in the championship game.

Morton became the backup for Roger Staubach for 1971, but when Staubach was injured in 1972, Morton returned to the starting lineup and passed for 2396 yards. The Cowboys finished with a 10-4 record and earned a wild card spot in the playoffs only to be beaten in the NFC title game by Washington.

Morton remained a backup with Dallas until the 1974 season, when he was traded to the New York Giants. He remained there two seasons, then moved to the AFC's Denver Broncos in 1977. Using his experience, Morton drove the Broncos to a 12-2 record and the AFC championship. Meanwhile, in the NFC, the Cowboys had turned in an impressive 12-2 record. The Super Bowl hype was built around the two old Dallas quarterbacking foes, Morton and Staubach, coming face to face. Played in the Louisiana Superdome, the game was the first Super Bowl held inside. The Cowboys quickly lowered the roof on Denver. Under heavy pressure, Morton threw first one interception, then another, which Dallas converted into scores, and the rout was on, ending 27-10.

Morton remained in Denver until 1982, when he retired. During his tenure, the Broncos again won the divisional title in 1978 and earned a wild card spot in the playoffs for 1979. But Morton never got another shot at the Super Bowl. Then again, the vast majority of quarterbacks never get a shot at one. Morton earned his rank among the league's elite.

Joe Namath

Joe Namath will forever be remembered as Broadway Joe, full of moxie and mouth, who directed the New York Jets' astounding victory over the Baltimore Colts in Super Bowl III.

He was the charismatic personality who happened upon the sport at the cusp of its evolution. Namath had been the long-haired, strong-armed quarterback shackled in the conservative offense of Alabama coach Bear Bryant in the early 1960s. Then in 1965, Namath collected the Orange Bowl Most Valuable Player Award and an unheard-of $400,000 bonus to sign with the Jets of the AFL. He immediately set out to wing the Jets to glory, and with the 1967 season, he became pro football's first 4000-yard passer. He completed 258 of 491 attempts for 4007 yards and 26 touchdowns, the only problem being that he also threw 28 interceptions. Yet even that seemed to suit the times.

The exciting 1968 season included the 'Heidi' game, the network gaffe that infuriated millions of television viewers but ultimately drew more attention to the raging competition in the AFL. Of course, Namath and the Jets were among the central characters, but they shared the lead with Daryle Lamonica and the perpetually dastardly Oakland Raiders. Aired by NBC, the 17 November match-up was a preview of the league championship. It was a darts match between Namath and Lamonica, an exchange of bulls-eyes featuring 71 passes and 19 penalties. Stretched by the style, the game was much longer than expected, developing into a 29-29 tie in the closing minutes. Then New York added a field goal for a 32-29 lead with a little over a minute left. Within seconds Lamonica pitched the Raiders to the Jets' 43 for a thrilling close.

That's when NBC officials abruptly switched to the scheduled broadcast of 'Heidi,' the children's classic.

Only viewers in the west, where it was 4 pm, saw the dramatic climax. The network waited more than an hour to flash the outcome across the bottom of the screen: Oakland 43, New York 32. Lamonica had thrown a 43-yard scoring pass to Charlie Smith with 43 seconds left, then the Jets fumbled the kickoff and Preston Ridelhuber picked up the ball and scored again.

The two teams resumed that scathing pace on 29 December in the AFC championship, played in the chill, swirling winds of New York's Shea Stadium. Oakland had gotten there by winning the Western Division with a 12-2 record, then eliminating the Kansas City Chiefs, 41-6, in a playoff; the Jets had zipped the East with 11 wins and 3 losses. The weather grounded both air attacks early in the championship. But Namath used his favorite receiver, Don Maynard, to work on Oakland's rookie cornerback George Atkinson, and a tight game ended with the Jets on top, 27-23.

The Jets were headed to the Super Bowl in Miami to meet the heavily favored Baltimore Colts. Namath's mouthing off to the press in the days before the Super Bowl seemed preposterous. 'The Jets will win on Sunday,' he told the Miami Touchdown Club three days before the game. 'I guarantee it.' In a more restrained manner, the Colts matched Namath's talk with haughtiness. Club and network (NBC had paid $2.5 million for broadcast rights) officials began planning the victory celebration in the Baltimore locker room. Colts owner Carroll Rosenbloom went so far as to invite Jets coach Weeb Ewbank to his victory party.

Namath and the Jets quickly established a ground game, with Matt Snell running effectively into the face of the Baltimore defense. The Jets shut down Baltimore's strong ground game and defended the pass ferociously. At the half, the Jets led, 7-0. In the third quarter Namath, troubled by a thumb injury, was replaced by veteran Babe Parilli, who continued the Jets' drive to a 16-7 victory. 'We didn't win on passing or running or defense,' said MVP Namath, who had completed 17 of 28 passes for 208 yards. 'We beat 'em in every phase of the game. If ever there was a world champion, this is it.'

Namath and the Jets returned to the AFL playoffs the next year and were bumped off by the eventual Super Bowl champions, the Kansas City Chiefs. After that, Super Joe's career became a struggle with his damaged knees. He remained with New York through a string of mostly mediocre seasons until 1977, when he joined the LA Rams. He retired from playing after a season of duty there and was inducted into the Hall of Fame in 1985.

Left: *Hall of Famer 'Broadway Joe' Namath.*

Opposite: *Namath steps up to drill one during Super Bowl III.*

Harry Newman

Harry Newman, an All-American from the University of Michigan, came into the NFL in 1933 and promptly found a spot as starting quarterback of the New York Giants. The Giants had struggled to a 4-6-2 record the year before, but with a bolstered roster and Newman's passing, they ran up an 11-3 record in 1933 and went to the title game.

For his part, Newman etched his name in the record books that year by leading the league in passing with 973 yards, a substantial accomplishment in the early years of the NFL. He completed 53 of 136 attempts and threw 11 touchdown passes against 17 interceptions.

Played at Wrigley Field before 30,000 fans, the 1933 title game between the Giants and the Chicago Bears was the NFL's first championship playoff. It developed into a seesaw affair. The great Bronko Nagurski moved the Bears along with his running and throwing, and 'Automatic' Jack Manders kicked three Chicago field goals. That was barely enough to counter a sterling effort by Harry Newman, who completed 12 of 20 passes for 201 yards and two touchdowns.

Late in the fourth quarter, it appeared New York would win, 21-16, until a quick touchdown by Chicago end Billy Karr gave the Bears a 23-21 lead. In the closing seconds, Newman threw to Dale Burnett, who broke into the open with Mel Hein running beside him, setting up a perfect lateral play for the winning score. But the legendary Red Grange tackled Burnett high and hard, pinning his arms from lateralling and saving the game for Chicago. Harry Newman's rookie year, a dream season, came close to having a championship ending.

Ken O'Brien

The New York Jets selected California-Davis quarterback Ken O'Brien in the first round of the 1983 draft, and by 1985 he was paying sizeable dividends as an investment.

His 1985 passing performance won him the AFC crown and helped his team revert from losers into playoff contenders. For the season, O'Brien completed 297 of 488 for 3888 yards and 25 touchdowns against only eight interceptions, giving him a league-high 96.2 rating, a 60.9 percent completion rate and only a 1.6 percent interception rate. What makes those statistics so incredible is that the young Jets quarterback ran up those numbers while playing behind an offensive line that allowed him to be sacked an NFL-record 62 times. After two straight losing years, the Jets finished 11-5 in 1985 and earned a wild card playoff bid. They were defeated in the first round by the New

England Patriots, 26-14, who were on their way to the Super Bowl. For his effort, O'Brien was named to the Pro Bowl.

In the third game of the next season, he outgunned Dan Marino and the Miami Dolphins in an incredible game, 51-45. With his team down 45-38 with 1:04 left, O'Brien drove his team 80 yards and tied the score with a 21-yard touchdown pass to Wesley Walker. Then he finished off the Dolphins in overtime with another strike to Walker, this time for 43 yards. On the day, O'Brien completed 29 of 43 for 479 yards and four touchdowns. In the tenth game, O'Brien completed an incredible 26 of 32 passes for 431 yards and four touchdowns and annihilated a strong Seattle team, 38-7, to bring the Jets to 9-1. When they beat the Colts the next week to move to pro football's best record at 10-1, the sportswriters began talking dynasty.

But the storybook season abruptly ended there, with the Jets' fall carrying all the speed of their rise. Over the last five games, all losses, O'Brien threw only two touchdown passes (he had thrown 23 in the first 11 games). Quite simply, his arm was worn out. Still, the Jets earned a wild card spot with a 10-6 record. Backup Pat Ryan replaced O'Brien for the playoffs and led them to a first-round win. The season ended with a 23-20 loss in overtime to the Browns.

O'Brien still finished the year with solid passing figures, 300 of 482 for 3690 yards, 25 touchdowns and a 85.8 rating. But the tired arm had led to a flurry of late-season interceptions, and he finished the year with 20. The future for the young quarterback seems rosy, particularly since he had learned a lesson about pacing.

Tommy O'Connell

In 1957, quarterback Tommy O'Connell of the Cleveland Browns set an incredible record. He completed 63 of 110 passes for 1229 yards, giving him an average gain of 11.17 yards, the highest in the history of the NFL. His nine touchdown passes meant that O'Connell had a touchdown percentage of 8.18 percent. The season had further distinction in that O'Connell won the NFL passing crown.

O'Connell had come to the forefront in the wake of Otto Graham's retirement after the 1955 season. For the 1956 season, Cleveland suffered its first losing record in its decade of existence. But O'Connell's 1957 performance helped propel the Browns back to the top. They won the Eastern Conference title with a 9-2-1 record. O'Connell and the Browns had a sensational rookie running back, Jim Brown, to help them in the NFL championship game against the Detroit Lions. But that didn't help as the Lions scored 17 quick points and went on to win, 59-14.

Still, O'Connell had made his way into the record books with his strong performance that year.

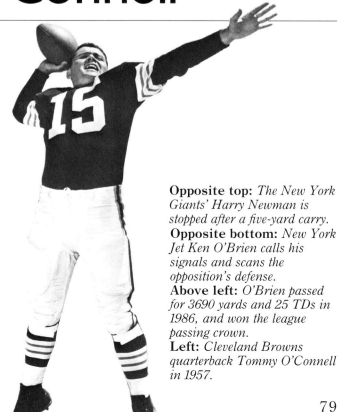

Opposite top: *The New York Giants' Harry Newman is stopped after a five-yard carry.*
Opposite bottom: *New York Jet Ken O'Brien calls his signals and scans the opposition's defense.*
Above left: *O'Brien passed for 3690 yards and 25 TDs in 1986, and won the league passing crown.*
Left: *Cleveland Browns quarterback Tommy O'Connell in 1957.*

Babe Parilli

In college, Vito 'Babe' Parilli played for coach Paul 'Bear' Bryant at the University of Kentucky. Combined, they led the Wildcats to their greatest seasons, including a Sugar Bowl win.

He was taken in the first round of the 1952 draft by the Green Bay Packers. From there he knocked around the pro leagues doing journeyman duty until a decade later in the spring of 1961, when the Oakland Raiders traded him to the Boston Patriots. There, Parilli would find his calling as a quarterback, completing 1140 passes, 132 of them for touchdowns, in six seasons of off-and-on play. He alternated with Butch Songin until 1963 when Parilli took control of the offense. Boston won the division with a 7-6-1 record, although the two previous seasons they hadn't been able to get in the playoffs with 9-4-1 records.

In a playoff game against the Buffalo Bills, Parilli threw two touchdown passes and the Pats won, 26-8, to advance to the AFL championship game against the San Diego Chargers. The fun ended there, however, as the Chargers won, 51-10.

Parilli had his best season in 1964, when he passed for 3465 yards and 31 touchdowns, both long-standing Patriots' records. On the strength of his performance, the Patriots ran out to a 10-3-1 record, including a late-season upset of the Buffalo Bills. But it wasn't enough to gain the playoffs.

Before the 1968 season, he was traded to the New York Jets where he became the backup and advisor to brash young Joe Namath. With Namath plagued by injuries, Parilli played frequently. His most important action came in the Jets' Super Bowl III victory over the Baltimore Colts. With the Jets leading 10-0 and Namath sidelined with a thumb injury, Parilli drove New York to a key field goal, eating up the clock while Colts Coach Don Shula paced nervously on the sidelines. It was a nice cameo appearance for a quarterback who had paid his dues.

Ace Parker

Opposite: *Babe Parilli saw most of his NFL action with the Boston Patriots from 1961 to 1968.*

Above: *Ace Parker of the Brooklyn Dodgers soars high off the ground versus the Redskins in 1941.*
Right: *Parker tears through the line for a 20-yard gain.*

As with most quarterbacks of his era, Clarence 'Ace' Parker could run, throw and kick, what the oldtimers call 'a legitimate triple threat.' But his ability as a kick returner took Parker to a level beyond that, to the realm of the 'quadruple threat.'

In his short career, which was interrupted by World War II, he was twice named the league's most valuable player. Parker came to the NFL in 1937 after leading Duke University to some of its greatest years. When he joined the Brooklyn Dodgers, they were perennial losers, but over the course of the next five seasons Parker's varied skills would be a major factor in building them into winners.

By 1940 the Dodgers' record was a splendid 8-3, giving them a second place finish behind the Washington Redskins. For 1941, Parker and the Dodgers finished the season 7-4, again good enough for a second-place divisional finish.

The franchise seemed poised on the verge of great-

ness, but World War II changed all that. Called to service, Parker didn't re-enter the league until 1945, when he joined the Boston Yanks. The next year, a new league formed, the All-American Football Conference, bringing with it an outbreak of bidding wars for the services of established NFL stars. Among those sought was Parker. For 1946, he signed a contract to play for the New York Yankees of the AAFC. The Yanks also picked up veteran NFL coach Ray Flaherty, whose Redskins teams had played in four NFL championship games and won two of them. The new league, however, would be dominated by Paul Brown and the Cleveland Browns.

Parker finished his playing career with the 1946 season. In 1972, he was inducted into the Hall of Fame.

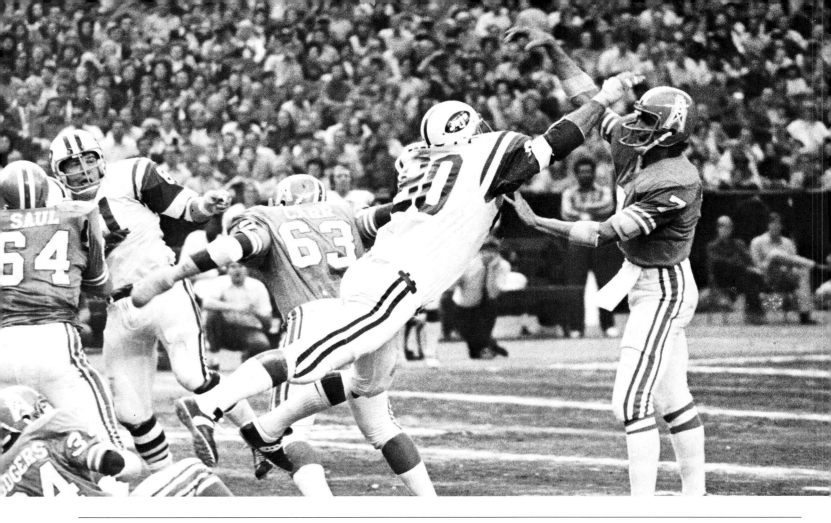

Dan Pastorini

Since the AFL-NFL merger in 1970, the Houston Oilers have compiled one of the league's worst records. They have, however, managed to make the playoffs three times in 17 years. Two of those three times, they were quarterbacked by Dan Pastorini.

Taken out of Santa Clara in the first round of the 1971 draft, Pastorini was seen as an important piece to the Houston puzzle. Another piece was added in 1975 when Bum Phillips was named coach, and yet another in 1978 when Texas running back Earl Campbell was drafted.

In 1975, Phillips' first year, Pastorini directed the Oilers to a 10-4 record, but was locked out of the playoffs because Pittsburgh and Cincinnati ruled the AFC Central with even better records. Pastorini's consolation came when he was named to the Pro Bowl after the season. But as for championships, the great Steelers would frustrate the Oilers throughout the rest of the decade.

With Campbell's running opening up the offense, Pastorini drove Houston to a 10-6 record and a wild card bid in 1978. During the season, Pastorini had suffered rib injuries and had to wear a flak jacket for protection. He didn't let that hamper him in the wild card game against Miami, as he completed 20 of 29 passes to lead Houston to a 17-9 win. The next week Pastorini

riddled the Patriots, completing 12 of 20 for 200 yards and three touchdowns for a 31-14 win. But the Pittsburgh defense hammered the Oilers and Pastorini in the playoffs, 34-5, and the Steelers moved on to their third Super Bowl title.

For 1979, Pastorini and Campbell again led the Oilers to a wild card slot with an 11-5 record. Both, however, were injured in a first-round victory over Denver. The next week, backup Houston quarterback Gifford Nielsen pushed the team to an upset of the San Diego Chargers, 17-14. Then, for the second straight year, Pastorini returned from injury to face the Steelers in the AFC championship. Going into the fourth quarter, the Steelers led 17-10. Pastorini threw a touchdown pass to receiver Mike Renfro that would have tied the game. But an official ruled that Renfro did not have possession of the ball before he went out of bounds. Instead, the Oilers settled for a fourth quarter field goal and still trailed, 17-13. From there, the Steelers added 10 points to win, 27-13. Pastorini had completed 19 of 28 passes for 203 yards against pro football's best defense.

In 1980, Pastorini was traded to the Oakland Raiders for quarterback Ken Stabler. Then, in the fifth game of 1980, Pastorini fractured his leg. He never returned to pro football's spotlight after that injury.

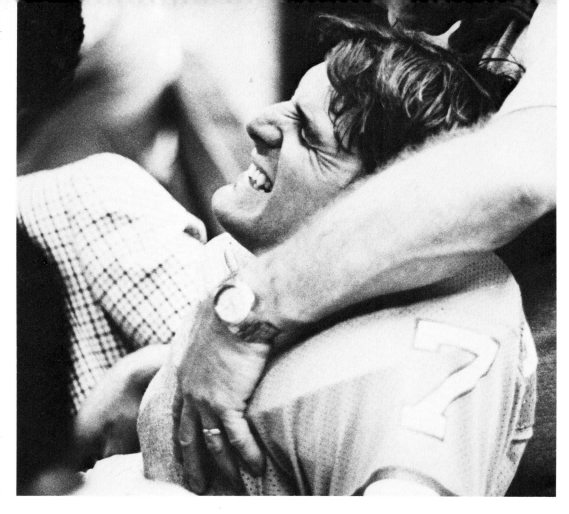

Milt Plum

Milt Plum, the Cleveland Browns star of the early 1960s, holds the distinction of having the highest rated passing season in the history of the NFL. In 1960, he rang up a 110.4, the best ever recorded: better than Sammy Baugh's 109.9 in 1945, better than Dan Marino's 108.9 in his record-shattering 1984 season.

For 1960, Plum won the NFL passing title by completing 151 of 250 passes for 2297 yards and 21 touchdowns. He threw only five interceptions. The next season, 1961, he again led the league in passing, completing 177 of 302 passes for 2416 yards and 18 touchdowns against only 10 interceptions.

In short, Plum was one of the most accurate passers in the history of pro football. For three consecutive seasons, 1959-61, he led the league in percentage of completions. Over the 1959 and 1960 seasons, he set an NFL record, later broken by Bart Starr of the Green Bay Packers, by attempting 208 passes without an interception.

With his fine performance, the Browns ran through a string of winning seasons, but they were never able to rise above a second-place finish in the NFL's Eastern Conference.

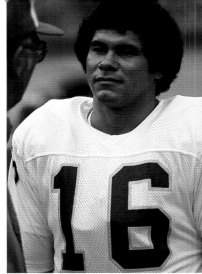

Left: *Veteran Jim Plunkett has quarterbacked the Raiders to two Super Bowl victories.* **Above:** *Plunkett is still going strong after more than 15 years in the NFL.*

Jim Plunkett

A Heisman winner out of Stanford, Jim Plunkett had won AFC Rookie of the Year honors in 1971 with New England, then drifted into anonymity. By 1980, he was the backup to Oakland's Dan Pastorini. He would have remained there if Pastorini hadn't suffered a fractured leg in the fifth game of the season. Plunkett took over from there, driving the Raiders to an 11-5 record and a wild card spot in the playoffs. There, they hammered Houston, 27-7, then eased by Brian Sipe and Cleveland, 14-12, and played a grand game against favored San Diego and Dan Fouts for the AFC title.

Plunkett, the backup, was suddenly taking a team to the Super Bowl. The Raiders' opponents were the Philadelphia Eagles, led by quarterback Ron Jaworski. Plunkett and the Raiders quickly established who had the magic in the Super Bowl. He completed 13 of 21 passes for 261 yards and three touchdowns to win MVP honors and the game, 27-10. Plunkett's 80-yard touchdown pass to Kenny King was the longest in Super Bowl history.

In 1983, Plunkett led the team to yet another Super Bowl upset. Joe Theismann and the Washington Redskins were rated a three-point favorite against the Raiders, who had throttled the Pittsburgh Steelers, 38-10, then repeated the act, 30-14, against the Seattle Seahawks of Chuck Knox in the AFC championship. Plunkett completed 17 of 24 passes for 214 yards in guiding the Raiders to the AFC win.

To say the least, Super Bowl XVIII left the Redskins stunned and elicited comparisons to their 73-0 loss to the Bears in 1940. Raiders' back Marcus Allen rushed for a Super Bowl record 191 yards, and the Raiders defense wrapped up the Washington offense for a 38-9 win. Plunkett ran the offense to perfection, completing 16 of 25 passes for 172 yards and a touchdown.

It might have seemed time to retire for many quarterbacks, but not Plunkett. At 39, he entered the NFL's 1987 season as the oldest player in the league. For distance men like Plunkett, it seems, there's always the chance for another title.

Tobin Rote

With two games left on the 1957 regular-season schedule, Detroit quarterback Bobby Layne was knocked out of play with a leg injury. His misfortune was the cue for backup Tobin Rote, who went out and seized his own little piece of greatness. Along with it, he brought Detroit another NFL championship.

With Rote at quarterback, the Lions tied San Francisco for the Western Conference regular season title (both teams had 8-4 records). But San Francisco, with Y A Tittle at quarterback, Hugh McElhenny in the backfield and R C Owens at receiver, was the favorite for the playoffs. The 49ers were playing at home, in Kezar Stadium, before a crowd of nearly 60,000. On Tittle's passing, the 49ers moved to an early 14-0 lead before the Lions momentarily found their offensive stride. Rote threw Steve Junker a three-yard touchdown pass to pull Detroit to 14-7. The 49ers answered with Tittle's third touchdown pass for a 21-7 lead, which they stretched to 27-7 early in the second half.

Somehow, with Rote guiding the offense and running back Tom 'The Bomb' Tracy providing the explosiveness, the Lions worked one of the NFL's greatest comebacks, eclipsing the staggering 49ers in the fourth quarter to win, 31-27. The victory sent the Lions into the title game against their old foes, the Cleveland Browns. Otto Graham had retired, but Paul Brown had a new weapon in rookie running back Jim Brown. The offensive spotlight, however, belonged to

Rote that day. The Detroit sub threw for 296 yards and four touchdown passes and ran for another as the Lions obliterated Cleveland, 59-14, for the NFL championship. It was the golden moment of Rote's career.

When the American Football League was started, he joined the San Diego Chargers, and in 1963 Rote won the league passing crown by throwing for 2510 yards and 20 touchdowns. That was enough to push the Chargers to the Western Division crown. In the AFL championship, Rote teamed with future Hall of Fame receiver Lance Alworth to blast the Boston Patriots, 51-10. On the day, Rote passed for two touchdowns and ran for another before turning the mop-up chores over to his backup, John Hadl, who assumed full-time duties the next season.

Below: *Tobin Rote of the Detroit Lions.*
Below left: *Rote, the San Diego Chargers' first quarterback, throws over the outstretched arm of the Bills' Tom Sestak (70) in the 1964 AFL title game in Buffalo.*

Frank Ryan

Frank Ryan is rated the sixteenth best passer in NFL history, having earned that distinction over his 13-year career by completing 1090 of 2133 passing attempts for 16,042 yards and 149 touchdowns. His career rating as a passer is 77.6.

Of all his grand moments in the game, Ryan's grandest came in 1964. He had pushed the Browns to the Eastern Conference title with a 10-3-1 record. But the Baltimore Colts, coached by Don Shula and quarterbacked by the great Johnny Unitas, had won the Western Conference with a 12-2 record and were considered substantial favorites to win the 1964 NFL championship.

The home crowd of nearly 80,000 had something to cheer about that afternoon in Cleveland Municipal Stadium. With a mix of man-for-man and zone pass defense, the Browns threw a net over Unitas' options and turned the first half into a scoreless defensive testing ground. The Colts threatened once early, but from there the day belonged to the underdogs.

In the second half, Cleveland's offensive performance caught up with the defense. Ryan ran the Colts' secondary crazy with a 27-point outburst that included three touchdown passes to veteran receiver Gary Collins to shut out the Colts, 27-0. For the day, Ryan threw for 206 yards, completing 11 of 18 passes. Collins caught five passes for 130 yards and the three scores.

The next year, Ryan again drove the team to the Eastern title with a 11-3 record. But for 1965, Green Bay coach Vince Lombardi had his dynasty back on track. In the championship game, Ryan came out firing and gave the Browns a 9-7 first quarter lead on a 17-yard scoring pass to Collins. In the end, the Packers' talent was too strong, the Lombardi appetite for victory too great. Green Bay won, 23-12. Despite that, Ryan had established his legend among the league's great quarterbacks.

Jay Schroeder

Out of UCLA, Jay Schroeder served as backup quarterback for the Washington Redskins until regular Joe Theismann suffered a career-ending broken leg in a November 1985 game against the New York Giants. Schroeder came on and led the Redskins to a come-from-behind victory that night. He went on to lead Washington to a 4-1 record to finish the season, but at 10-6, the Redskins missed the playoffs.

In 1986, Schroeder's first full year as a starter, he reached an incredible milestone, becoming one of only nine quarterbacks in the history of the league to pass for more than 4000 yards in a season. He completed 276 of 541 attempts for 4109 yards and 22 touchdowns against 22 interceptions. His performance helped Washington to a 12-4 record and a wild card spot in the playoffs. Once there, he quarterbacked the Skins past the LA Rams, 19-7, in the first round, then engineered an upset of the defending world champion Chicago Bears in the second, 27-13. In the NFC championship game, the overpowering defense of the New York Giants and the chill winds of Giants Stadium exposed Schroeder's inexperience in a 17-0 domination.

Schroeder was named to the Pro Bowl after the season in recognition of his remarkable performance.

Opposite top: *Frank Ryan of the Cleveland Browns after tossing five touchdowns and running for one in a 52-25 win over the Giants for the NFL East title on 12 December 1964.*
Opposite bottom: *Ryan with Browns head coach Blanton Collier (middle) and fullback Jim Brown (right) in 1965.*
Right: *The Washington Redskins' Jay Schroeder went to the Pro Bowl following the 1986 season after passing for over 4000 yards and leading the Redskins to the NFC championship.*

Phil Simms

When the Giants selected Phil Simms out of Morehead State in the first round of the 1979 draft, they were a franchise struggling to regain respectability. By 1981, the Giants had earned a wild card playoff spot, but had fallen to last place in their division by 1983. Then for the next two years, Simms rebounded them to wild card spots. In October 1985, he completed 40 of 62 passes against Cincinnati for 513 yards, the second highest single-game total in the history of the league. Then after the season, he was selected to play in the Pro Bowl, where he earned MVP honors by throwing three touchdown passes to lead the NFC in a come-from-behind win, 28-24.

In 1986 Simms lived the great dream of all pro quarterbacks: he took his team to the Super Bowl, and once there, he put on one of the finest passing performances in the history of the game. In leading the New York Giants to a 39-20 victory over the Denver Broncos in Super Bowl XXI, Simms completed 22 of 25 passes to set a Super Bowl record for completion percentage, a whopping 88.0 (far beyond the 73.5 percent turned in by Cincinnati's Ken Anderson in 1982). Simms' three touchdown passes took the kick out of the Broncos and assured him the game MVP trophy.

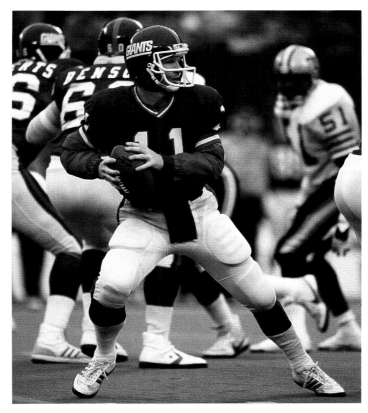

Brian Sipe

From 1974 to 1983, Brian Sipe was the heart of the Cleveland Browns' offense. In that time, he set club passing records for career yardage (23,713) and touchdowns (154).

The challenge of his career was to lift the once-mighty Browns from the dregs of the AFC Central Division. By 1976, he had helped make them winners again, and in 1980, he took them all the way to the division crown.

For four seasons – 1979, 1980, 1981 and 1983 – he threw for more than 3000 yards. His 1980 performance set a new single-season passing yardage record of 4132 yards (which would later be broken by San Diego's Dan Fouts). On the year, he threw 30 touchdown passes against 14 interceptions. Sipe's great year, however, died in a last-second playoff loss to the Oakland Raiders, the eventual Super Bowl champions. Sipe was named to the Pro Bowl after the season.

Opposite top: *New York Giants quarterback Phil Simms, MVP for both the 1986 Pro Bowl and Super Bowl XXI.*
Opposite bottom: *Simms hurls one against the LA Rams.*

Below: *Cleveland Browns quarterback Brian Sipe flies through the air as he picks up nine yards running the ball in a game versus the Cincinnati Bengals in 1981.*

Norm Snead

The Washington Redskins needed an instant quarterback, so they selected Norm Snead out of Wake Forest University in the first round of the 1961 draft. As they hoped, he fit the bill perfectly, setting the record his first season for passes attempted by a rookie (375) and yards gained passing by a rookie (2337). Both records have since been broken.

But in 1963, the Redskins had an opportunity to obtain veteran Philadelphia quarterback Sonny Jurgensen, so they sent Snead to the Eagles. There, he racked up passing totals to rank him among the game's greats. Snead ranks eleventh on the all-time list for passes attempted (4353), twelfth on the all-time list for passes completed (2273), tenth in yards passing (30,797) and fourteenth in touchdown passes (196).

For the most part, his career was a struggle to lift the Eagles on the strength of his passing skills. Their best season under his guidance was a 9-5 record in 1966. Playing for the New York Giants in 1972, Snead won the NFC passing crown by completing 196 of 325 attempts for 2307 yards and 17 touchdowns against 12 interceptions. With that effort, the Giants finished with an 8-6 record, and Snead was named to the Pro Bowl. It was a nice touch at the close of a long career.

Ken Stabler

Ken Stabler made his NFL debut in the 23 December 1972 'Immaculate Reception' game between the Oakland Raiders and the Pittsburgh Steelers. Stabler replaced Oakland quarterback Daryle Lamonica on the Raiders' last-ditch drive. With 1:13 left, Stabler, who would come to be known by the nickname 'Snake,' scampered 30 yards for a touchdown and a 7-6 Oakland lead.

It was only the second touchdown allowed by the Steelers over five games, but it appeared to be enough to beat them. Then with 22 seconds left, Steelers quarterback Terry Bradshaw threw the famous 'Immaculate Reception' to give Pittsburgh the last-second victory. The loss was crushing for Oakland, but it gave the Raiders a preview of the player who would finally help them realize their greatness.

The next year Stabler quarterbacked Oakland to the AFC championship game, only to see the defending world champion Miami Dolphins earn the Super Bowl ticket, 27-10. The following year, 1974, Stabler and the Raiders produced a repeat performance, but in the AFC championship game he threw three interceptions to go along with 271 yards passing and Pittsburgh won, 24-13. Then in 1975, the same scenario developed, with the Raiders again losing to Pittsburgh in the AFC title game, this time 16-10, as Stabler threw for 246 yards and two interceptions.

Finally, that great moment came in 1976, when the Raiders blasted to a 13-1 regular season record behind Stabler's 2737 yards passing and Mark van Eeghen's 1012 yards rushing. After a close game against New England in the playoffs (Stabler drove the Raiders to two fourth-quarter touchdowns to win, 24-21), John Madden's bunch dethroned the reigning Steelers in the AFC championship, 24-7. Stabler completed 10 of 16 passes for 88 yards and two touchdowns.

Figured to be a close game, their Super Bowl match-up with Minnesota proved to be a mere formality. Oakland won, 32-14, as Stabler completed 12 of 19 passes for 180 yards and a touchdown, with no interceptions. Clarence Davis had rushed for 137 yards, and Fred Biletnikoff had won the MVP award with four catches for 77 yards, but the day more than any other Super Bowl had been a team victory.

Stabler couldn't produce another championship the next season, but on Christmas Eve, he gave the football world a bag of thrills with a double sudden-death overtime game against Bert Jones and the Baltimore Colts. Stabler hit 20 of 41 passes for 345 yards and three touchdowns, all to tight end Dave Casper, including the 10-yard winner in the sixth period of play for a final score of 37-31.

The Raiders were nipped in the AFC championship game the next week, 20-17, by Denver. Stabler never

Opposite: *Norm Snead of the Eagles sets to pass behind good protection against the Lions in 1968.*

Above: *Oakland's Ken Stabler with head coach John Madden at the close of the Raiders' 32-14 win over Minnesota in Super Bowl XI.*
Right: *Stabler captured AFC passing crowns in 1973 and 1976.*

took Oakland's black and silver troops back to the playoffs. Instead, he finished his playing career with stints in Houston and New Orleans.

A product of Bear Bryant's Alabama program, Stabler ranks sixteenth on the all-time list for passes attempted (3793); thirteenth for passes completed (2270); fifteenth for passing yardage (27,938); and sixteenth for touchdown passes (194). His career pass completion percentage of 59.85 is the third highest in the history of the league. In 1973 and 1976 he won the AFC passing crown. Over his career, he threw for 2641 yards in playoff games, also the third highest in the history of the league. In 13 playoff games, he threw 19 touchdown passes, another third-place ranking in league history. In 10 consecutive playoff games, Stabler threw at least one touchdown pass, a statistic unequalled by any other pro quarterback.

Bart Starr

Left: *Green Bay Packer Bart Starr entered the Hall of Fame in 1977.*
Right: *Starr passed his way to Green Bay club records for touchdown passes and yardage thrown.*
Opposite: *Starr fades back in a game against the Baltimore Colts. He went on to play for the Packers until 1971, and later coached his former team.*

A quarterback out of the University of Alabama, Bart Starr joined the Green Bay Packers in 1956, and like the rest of the team, he suffered through three years of losing until Vince Lombardi was named coach. From there, the path of Starr's career, as well as that of his teammates, was paved with championships – five NFL titles and two Super Bowl trophies. In the history of pro football, never has there been such a spectacular alignment. Starr was a great quarterback fortunate enough to play on a great team.

After taking over in 1959, Lombardi drove his team to the NFL championship game against the Philadelphia Eagles in 1960. Starr ran a passing game that completed 21 of 35 passes for 178 yards and a touchdown, but the veteran Eagles slipped past the young Packers, 17-13. For 1961, the Packers scored a league-leading 391 points and won the NFL Western crown with a 11-3 record. In the championship game against the New York Giants, Starr was masterful, completing 10 of 19 for 164 yards and three touchdowns as Green Bay won, 37-0.

The franchise only ripened the next season, finishing off the Western competition with a 13-1 record and meeting the Giants again for the NFL title. Fighting gusting winds, Starr completed nine of 21 passes for 96 yards and no interceptions as the Packers claimed their second title, 16-7. For the 1965 NFL title game against Cleveland, Starr completed 10 of 19 attempts for 128 yards with an interception. The passing game bolstered a strong ground attack, and the Packers took home a third NFL title, 23-12.

Dallas and Don Meredith became the challengers for 1966, and Starr helped subdue them with one of his finest passing performances. He completed 19 of 28 passes for 304 yards and three touchdowns against no interceptions for a 34-27 win. The prize of that game was to face the Kansas City Chiefs, the AFL champions, in the first Super Bowl. Led by Len Dawson, the Chiefs provided a stiff challenge to the heavily favored Packers in the first half, but the defense and Starr's passing finally subdued them in the second, 35-10. Starr completed 16 of 23 attempts for 250 yards and two touchdowns against one interception.

For 1967, the Packers again found the Dallas Cowboys and Meredith in their path. That NFL championship game will forever be known as the Ice Bowl. With the game time temperature at Milwaukee's Lambeau Field a wicked 13 below zero, the Packers skated to an early 14-0 lead on two Starr touchdown passes to receiver Boyd Dowler. The scoring was as frozen as the weather until the early moments of the fourth quarter when the Cowboys took a 17-14 lead on a 50-yard halfback option pass from Dan Reeves to Lance Rentzel. With 4:54 on the clock, Starr jumpstarted the Packers offense. Between them and a third consecutive NFL championship stood 68 yards, the cold, and one of football's best defenses.

First there was a six-yard gain by running back

Donny Anderson. Then reserve running back Chuck Mercein sliced off tackle for a first down. Starr next threw to Boyd Dowler at the Dallas 42. Just as the momentum crested, the Cowboys threw Anderson for a nine-yard loss. Before the defense could celebrate, Starr answered with two quick completions to Anderson for a first down at the 30, with 1:35 left. Mercein then got open beyond the linebackers on the left, and after Starr found him with a pass, raced to the 11, where he ran out of bounds to stop the clock. On the next play, Mercein dashed off tackle for eight yards to the three.

There, on a plane of ice, the two teams played out one of pro football's classic dramas. Two rushes by Anderson netted two yards and a first down. On third down and goal at the one with 0:16 left, Starr called for a dive between guard Jerry Kramer and center Ken Bowman. But rather than risk a handoff, Starr made

the play a keeper, and landed over the goal line.

The Packers had won their third straight NFL championship, 21-17. Starr had completed 14 of 24 attempts for 191 yards and two touchdowns and had run over the winning score. Among the spoils was a trip to Super Bowl II against the Oakland Raiders in Miami's Orange Bowl. Starr drilled the Raiders, completing 13 of 24 for 202 yards and a touchdown. Lombardi's troops claimed their second Super Bowl trophy, 33-14.

Although much of the team would retire after that spectacular season and coach Lombardi resigned, Starr would remain with the team until 1971, setting club records for yardage and touchdown passes. He ranks twelfth in the NFL's all-time passers with an 80.5 career rating. In 16 years, he completed 1808 of 3149 attempts for 23,718 yards and 152 touchdowns against 138 interceptions.

In 1977 Starr was inducted into the Hall of Fame.

Roger Staubach

Roger Staubach won the Heisman trophy as a running quarterback for Navy in 1963, and because he had a six-year commitment to the service, most pro football teams passed him over in the 1964 draft. The Dallas Cowboys finally selected him in the tenth round, which at the time seemed like a gamble.

He began by sharing playing time with Craig Morton. Eventually, Staubach would gain fame as the game's last-second miracle worker. Over his career, Staubach would lead Dallas to 23 come-from-behind wins, 14 of them coming in the final two minutes.

In his decade with Dallas, he was the driving force that pushed the franchise to 10 winning seasons and two world titles. For 1970, the Cowboys and their system of revolving quarterbacks rolled to the NFC crown. With Morton taking the snaps, they eliminated John Brodie and the San Francisco 49ers in the conference title game and battled the Colts in Super Bowl V before losing on a last-second field goal, 16-13.

For the next season, Coach Tom Landry settled on Staubach as the team's quarterback. The 6-foot-2, 190-pounder responded by leading the NFC in passing and taking the Cowboys back to the Super Bowl. There he took them one giant step further – to their first championship. On their way, the Cowboys again turned back John Brodie and the 49ers in the NFC championship game. Showing the balance of his skills, Staubach rushed for 55 yards and completed nine of 18 pass attempts for 103 yards. Don Shula's Miami Dolphins were the opponents in Super Bowl VI. The Cowboys, behind Staubach's passing (completing 12 of 19 for 119 yards and two touchdowns) and Duane Thomas' 95 yards rushing, dispatched the Dolphins, 24-3.

The Cowboys' plans would be frustrated over the next three seasons as the Washington Redskins and the Minnesota Vikings represented the NFC in the Super Bowl. In 1975, Dallas made the playoffs as a wild card team, laced with rookies and carrying a 10-4 record into the first round against Minnesota at Metropolitan Stadium in Minneapolis.

In the fourth quarter against the Cowboys, the Vikings put together a drive to take a 14-10 lead. With 37 seconds left, Dallas had a first down at the 50. When the next pass fell incomplete, Staubach threw it long again, to cornerback Nate Wright. The pass was short, bringing receiver Drew Pearson back from the end zone to catch it. As he moved to the ball, Wright fell, or as the Vikings claimed, he was knocked down by offensive interference. Pearson caught the ball at the five, clutched it to his waist, then felt it slipping away as he fell into the end zone. With the ball pinned awkwardly at his hip, Pearson glanced around for penalty flags. There were none, only the dead silence of Metropolitan Stadium. The play became enshrined as 'Hail

Left: *Roger 'The Dodger' Staubach, a 1985 Hall of Fame enshrinee.*
Opposite top: *Staubach of the Cowboys hands off to running back Calvin Hill. Ice-cool under pressure, he led Dallas to many come-from-behind victories.*
Opposite bottom: *The Dallas Cowboys captured two Super Bowls (VI and XII) under the guidance of Staubach.*

Mary,' and has become over the years one of the game's hallowed moments.

From that first-round miracle, Dallas went on to claim the NFC title, blowing past the Los Angeles Rams, 37-7, in the championship game as Staubach completed 16 of 26 for 200 yards and four touchdown passes. Super Bowl X brought a letdown for Staubach. He completed 15 of 24 passes for 204 yards and two touchdowns, but he also threw three interceptions. Adding those gifts to their already bulging good fortunes, the Pittsburgh Steelers eased to a 21-17 win. Still, the game wasn't over until they intercepted Staubach's final Hail Mary attempt.

The Cowboys and Staubach again won their division the next season, 1976, but were bumped from the playoffs by Los Angeles. If anything, that doubled their determination for 1977. They blasted to the division crown with a 12-2 record, then wrecked Chicago and Minnesota in the NFC playoffs, and devastated the Denver Broncos in Super Bowl XII, 27-10. With Staubach completing 17 of 25 attempts for 183 yards and a touchdown, the Cowboys had their second world title. They got a shot at a third title the next year against Pittsburgh in Super Bowl XIII. The game was hardly a masterpiece as a series of miscues and turnovers left Dallas trailing, 21-17, going into the fourth period. Then the downslide became an avalanche when the Steelers took a 35-17 lead with a little over six minutes left. But the game was not over yet.

Staubach trotted onto the field, drove the Cowboys 89 yards and scored to make it 35-24 with 2:27 left. Then they recovered the onsides kick, and eight plays later, Staubach hit Butch Johnson with a four-yard pass for a 35-31 score with 0:22 on the clock. This time, however, the Steelers' Rocky Bleier covered the onsides kick, robbing Staubach of the chance to work his magic one more time. He wouldn't have a greater moment until the 1979 season, when he led a wild comeback to knock the Washington Redskins out of a postseason berth.

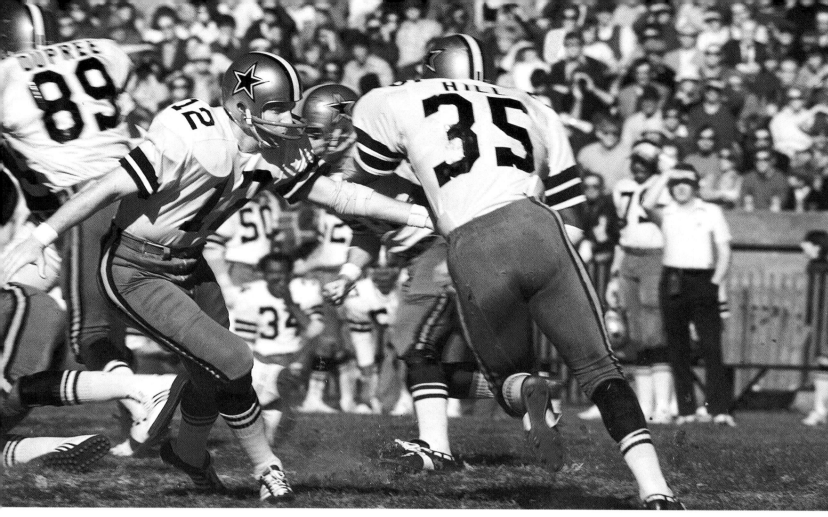

Staubach called Dallas' 35-34 come-from-behind win over Washington in December 1979 the most exciting game he ever played as a Cowboy. Going into the final game of the 1979 season at Texas Stadium, both Washington and Dallas had 10-5 records. If the Redskins won the game, they had the NFC East title. If they lost, their season would end, because the Chicago Bears had a points advantage for the wild card spot.

The Redskins powered and finessed their way to a 17-0 second quarter lead, seemingly enough to put the game away. Even Staubach had never come back from such a deficit. The Cowboys calmly put together a scoring drive midway through the period, and then as time wound down, they added another, albeit a bit more frantically. With 0:09 on the clock, Staubach threw Preston Pearson a 26-yard touchdown pass to end the half, setting the stage for the Cowboys' third period drive to give them the lead, 21-17. Washington awakened with another 17-point outburst to leave the Cowboys trailing 34-28 with 1:47 on the clock. Staubach used 60 seconds to get to the Washington 8. On the next play, he lofted the ball to Tony Hill in the corner of the end zone, just beyond the reach of defensive back Lemar Parrish. Rafael Septien's extra point was the winner, 35-34.

Staubach was inducted into the Hall of Fame in 1985. With an 83.4 career rating, he ranks fifth on the NFL's all-time passing list. In 11 seasons, he completed 1685 of 2958 attempts for 22,700 yards, 153 touchdown passes and two world titles.

Fran Tarkenton

Fran Tarkenton is what you might call the ultimate quarterback, lacking only the ultimate prize: a Super Bowl championship. Over an 18-year NFL career that spanned stints with the Minnesota Vikings, then the New York Giants, then the Vikings again, Tarkenton rang up the statistics that make him the most prodigious passer in the history of pro football.

He heads the all-time rankings of yardage gained (47,003), passes completed (3686), passes attempted (6467), and touchdown passes (342). He ranks third on the all-time interception list with 266 (George Blanda is tops with 277).

He came to the Vikings, the NFL's new franchise, in 1961 out of the University of Georgia, and he suffered with the team all the growing pains that expansion clubs suffer. Still, they won three games that first year, and by the 1964 season, the Vikings turned in a winner at 8-5-1.

For 1967, Tarkenton was traded to the New York Giants, where he struggled with a rebuilding team until the Vikings reacquired him for the 1972 season. Tarkenton pushed the team to a 12-2 record and the NFC Central Division title for 1973. He threw two touchdown passes to John Gilliam to beat Washington in the first round of the playoffs, then ran the control offense over Dallas, 27-10, to claim the NFC championship. The Miami Dolphins, however, dominated Super Bowl VII, 24-7, setting up a pattern that would haunt Tarkenton for the rest of his career.

The Vikings won the Central again in 1974 with a 10-4 record, and then struggled against Pittsburgh's defense in Super Bowl IX before losing 16-6. After a playoff loss to Dallas in 1975, the Vikings came back strong again in 1976, running off an 11-2-1 record and nailing Washington and Los Angeles in the NFC playoffs. Again, Super Bowl XI was an exercise in frustration. The Oakland Raiders dominated, 32-14. Tarkenton left the field in frustration after fumbling in the second half.

Injuries kept Tarkenton out of the NFC championship game in 1977, but the Dallas Cowboys shoved the Vikings aside there, 24-7. Minnesota won the Division the next season, Tarkenton's last, but his final Super Bowl hopes died in the first round of the playoffs at the hands of Los Angeles, 34-10.

Three times Tarkenton had taken a fine team to within one game of the world championship. That and his passing records would have to be his consolation. For those great achievements, Tarkenton was voted into the Hall of Fame in 1986.

Above right: *Vikings quarterback Fran Tarkenton eludes the Falcons' Claude Humphrey.*

Right: *Tarkenton played for the Giants from 1967 to 1971.* **Opposite top:** *Joe Theismann, Redskins quarterback.*

Joe Theismann

An academic All-American and two year starter at Notre Dame, Joe Theismann finished second in the 1970 Heisman trophy voting behind Jim Plunkett.

He came to the Washington Redskins in 1974, where he joined the quarterback sweepstakes with veterans Sonny Jurgensen and Billy Kilmer. Filling an early role as a utility player, Theismann did duty as a punt returner for the Redskins. With the retirement of the veterans, he assumed the starting role in Washington and spent the next half decade battling Roger Staubach and the Dallas Cowboys. In 1979, Staubach retired, and after a shakeup in Redskins coaching, Theismann and company were primed in 1982. The only interfering factor was the early season strike by the NFL players' union. With that resolved in mid-season, Washington posted an 8-1 record and Theismann claimed the NFC passing crown by completing 161 of 252 attempts for 2033 yards and 13 touchdowns against nine interceptions.

In the NFC championship game with the Dallas Cowboys, Theismann was a picture of proficiency, completing 12 of 20 passes for 150 yards and a touchdown as Washington advanced to Super Bowl XVII, 31-17. The opponents were the Miami Dolphins with their Killer Bees stinging defense. Theismann threw for two touchdowns and teamed with 32-year-old run-ning back John Riggins to defeat Miami 27-17, Washington's first championship since 1942.

Theismann was named to the Pro Bowl, and continued that pace the next season, 1983, running the Redskins to a 14-2 record and shattering the team total offense record with 541 points. In the playoffs, they bombed the Rams 51-7 and nipped the San Francisco 49ers, 24-21, in the NFC championship game as Theismann passed for 229 yards and a touchdown. Overwhelming favorites for Super Bowl XVIII against the Los Angeles Raiders, the Redskins instead were overwhelming disappointments, losing 38-9.

Theismann salvaged part of a fine season in the Pro Bowl, where he was named Most Valuable Player after completing 21 of 27 passes for 242 yards and three touchdowns in leading the NFC to an incredible 45-3 win. He returned the next season and struggled somewhat before suffering a career-ending broken leg in the eleventh game, a Monday night meeting with the New York Giants.

A talkative, gutsy fighter, Theismann fared well statistically over the years. He ranks eighteenth in the NFL's all-time passing ratings. Over 12 years, he completed 2044 of 3602 attempts for 25,206 yards and 160 touchdowns against 138 interceptions, for a 77.4 career rating.

Tommy Thompson

Opposing defenses often attempted to 'blind-side' Philadelphia Eagles' quarterback Tommy Thompson because he was legally blind in his left eye. When opponents blitzed, they often came from his poor field of vision, but they never quite found a way to make that strategy work for long. Thompson led the Eagles to three NFL title games and helped them carry home two championships.

Having played college ball at the University of Tulsa, Thompson played for the Eagles in the early 1940s, then like many other players of his era, had his career interrupted by World War II. He rejoined the team after the war and played a big role in getting the franchise on the winning track. For 1947, the Eagles won the Eastern Division and met the Chicago Cardinals in the NFL title game. Thompson played magnificently in the title game, completing 27 of 44 passes for 297 yards, then a title game record, but the Cards broke a series of long runs to edge Philly, 28-21.

For 1948, Thompson led the NFL in passing, completing 141 of 246 passes for 1965 yards and 25 touchdowns against only 11 interceptions. With Thompson running the show, the Eagles had the same kind of year, winning the division with a 9-2-1 record. Bad weather helped the Eagles play defense in their championship rematch with the Cards, as Philly won, 7-0, despite Thompson's two of 12 passing in the chill winds and snow.

The Eagle magic continued in 1949. Thompson ran the team to the Eastern Division crown with 364 points of offense and an 11-1 record. Their opponents were the equally potent Los Angeles Rams, who had erupted for a league-record 466 points. Steve Van Buren was the power in the Eagles' ground game, and in the championship game, he sloshed through a Los Angeles downpour for 191 yards rushing on 31 carries. Thompson ran the offense and threw a 31-yard touchdown pass to take Philadelphia to a second championship, 14-0.

In the late 1970s, he returned to Philadelphia for a team reunion to find that his teammates had scheduled a visit for him to a local eye surgeon. Thompson underwent treatment and regained a portion of the vision he had lost as a child.

Y A Tittle

After playing 13 seasons with Baltimore and San Francisco, Y A Tittle was traded to the hastily rebuilt New York Giants in 1961. In 1962, he threw 33 touchdowns to lead the league, and the next year he retained the crown by throwing a league-record 36. Three times he led the Giants to the NFL championship game, and three times Tittle was denied. It seemed that when he needed touchdown passes the most, he couldn't find the range.

The Packers stood in his path in 1961 and 1962. Kramer, Dowler, Starr, Taylor and Hornung put on a show in the 1961 title game, smashing New York, 37-0, for Green Bay's first championship since 1944. The next year, the Packers worked their power again, snuffing Tittle and the Giants, 16-7, for Lombardi's second championship.

Then, in 1963, Tittle and the Giants met The Monsters of the Midway, George Halas' Chicago Bears, for the championship. The Bears' trademark was their defense, directed by assistant coach George Allen. The Giants, of course, cornered the offensive market, averaging better than 32 points a game with Tittle

throwing for more than 3100 yards. He would, however, have trouble de-icing his air attack in Chicago's eight degree weather and lashing winds.

Tittle was injured in the first half but returned in the third quarter to protect a 10-7 lead. His misfortune was to throw an interception that led to the Bears' second score and a 14-10 lead, the winning margin. Twice after that the limping Tittle drove the Giants downfield only to be intercepted each time. The game ended with his fifth interception.

Despite the absence of a championship ring, there was ample evidence of Tittle's spirit and ability. Out of LSU, he broke in with the Baltimore Colts of the All-America Football Conference in 1948 and fought pro football's good fight for 17 seasons. In that time, he completed 2427 of 4395 passing attempts for 33,070 yards and 242 touchdown passes.

His highlights include throwing seven touchdown passes against the Redskins on 28 October 1962 (he also completed 27 of 39 passes on the day for 505 yards) and winning the NFL passing crown in 1963.

In 1971, Tittle was inducted into the Hall of Fame.

Opposite: *Pittsburgh Steelers quarterback Tommy Thompson is upended after a five-yard gain against the Redskins on 3 November 1940.*
Above: *Hall of Famer Y A Tittle of the New York Giants led the league in touchdown passes in 1962 and 1963, with 33 and 36, respectively.*
Right: *Tittle throws a 14-yard touchdown strike to Frank Gifford in the 1963 championship game versus Chicago.*

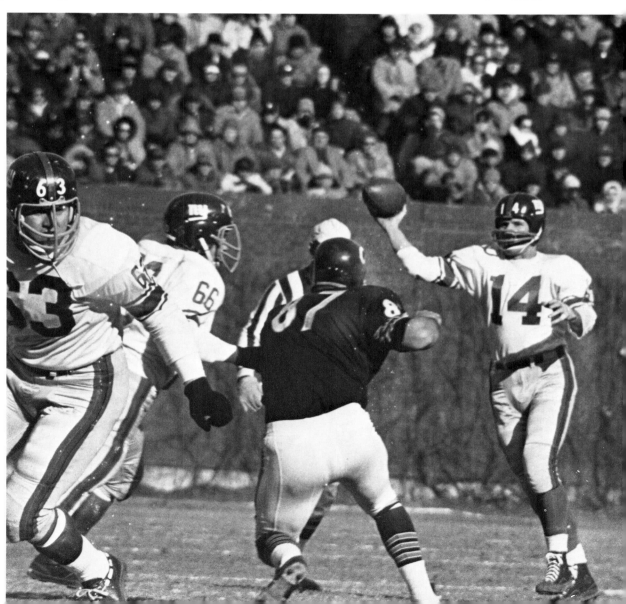

Richard Todd

A first-round draft pick out of the University of Alabama in 1976, Richard Todd joined the New York Jets as the heir apparent to Joe Namath's legacy. While he never came close to filling Broadway's white shoes, Todd did leave his mark on pro football.

His greatest success came in 1981 and 1982 when he took the Jets to the playoffs. For 1981, he led the team to a 10-5-1 record and a wild card playoff spot. New York lost in the first round, 31-27, to the Buffalo Bills. The next season, 1982, was shortened by a players' strike, but Todd still pushed the jets to a 6-3 record and a strong showing in the 'Super Bowl tournament.' There, he pulled the trigger as New York gunned down Ken Anderson and the Cincinnati Bengals, 44-17. Next, the Jets took on the LA Raiders, who had the best record in the AFC at 8-1. With Todd at the controls, New York pulled off the upset, 17-14.

The magic ended against Miami in the AFC championship, as the Dolphin pass rush harassed Todd into throwing three interceptions. One of his finest performances came against the Los Angeles Rams in a 1983 overtime game, when he completed 37 of 50 passes for 446 yards and two touchdowns.

He was traded to the New Orleans Saints in 1984, and his career shifted to backup duties. However, he holds the distinction of having completed more passes in a game than any quarterback in the history of the sport. He achieved that on 21 September 1980 against the San Francisco 49ers when he connected 42 times.

Above: *Richard Todd's 42 completions for the New York Jets against San Francisco in 1980 is an NFL record.*
Below: *Todd takes off, with Lawrence Taylor of the New York Giants in hot pursuit, in a 1981 game.*

Opposite: *Denver Broncos quarterback Frank Tripucka hits his hole during a 32-10 win over the New York Titans on 30 September 1962.*

Frank Tripucka

Frank Tripucka was one of the better journeyman quarterbacks in pro football during the 1950s and 1960s. He came out of Notre Dame in 1949 and did time in the NFL and Canadian Football League before finding a home with the Denver Broncos of the AFL. In all, he played 15 seasons of pro ball, completing 1707 of 3126 attempts for 22,701 yards and a career completion percentage of 54.6.

In 1960, he set a Denver club record by throwing for 24 touchdown passes in a season. Nearly two decades later, that record was still standing despite the best efforts of Craig Morton and John Elway. Unfortu-

nately, he also set a pro football record for interceptions that season (34) that would stand until 1962 when George Blanda, who was with the Houston Oilers at that time, threw an incredible 42.

One of Tripucka's biggest seasons was 1962. Against Buffalo in September, he completed 29 of 56 attempts for 447 yards and two touchdowns. A month later he threw five touchdown passes in a game. Both marks are Denver club records.

After his retirement, club officials in Denver retired Tripucka's number 18, making him one of only 18 quarterbacks in the NFL to hold that distinction.

Johnny Unitas

In many observers' eyes, Johnny Unitas is the greatest quarterback of all time. He ranks only fourteenth on the all-time list of league passers with a 78.2 rating. He threw 290 touchdown passes over his 18-year career, but he also threw 253 interceptions. He completed 2830 of 5186 passing attempts for 40,239 yards. Yet Fran Tarkenton threw more passes, completed more, connected on more touchdown passes and had nearly 7000 more yards passing. And not once in his 18 years of playing did Unitas lead the league in passing.

Faced with such statistical evidence, the true Unitas admirers will tell you to forget the numbers. Unitas was the most daring passer in the history of pro football, a quarterback without fear. In 47 consecutive NFL games, he threw a touchdown pass, nearly double what any other quarterback has accomplished.

He had been a ninth-round draft pick out of the University of Louisville in 1955, and had been cut by the Pittsburgh Steelers. The Baltimore Colts dug him up in 1956 when their regular, George Shaw, was injured. The next season, 1957, Coach Weeb Ewbank watched Johnny U become the league MVP. Despite the award, Unitas was still a reasonably well-kept secret the next season. Then came the 1958 title game.

Oldtimers will recall that the New York Giants were overwhelming favorites. The Giants had given up a league-low 183 points and outlasted Cleveland three times to win the Eastern Conference title. The Colts

had their share of talent as well. Unitas sent most of his mail to rangy, precise Raymond Berry, the split end. L G Dupre and Alan 'The Horse' Ameche were the power in the backfield. Lenny Moore was the flanker/halfback.

New York had won the regular-season contest between the two teams, and Baltimore hadn't beaten the Giants since 1954. Furthermore, the setting for their epic collision was Yankee Stadium, filled with 64,175 truly lucky fans lusting for the thud of the Giants' defense. A few million more tuned in on television.

At halftime the Colts had a 14-3 advantage, but the Giants made a great comeback and regained the lead, 17-14, early in the fourth quarter. With 1:56 left, the Colts were pinned at their 14. But Unitas found a spark and turned it into a flame. On third and 10, he passed to Lenny Moore for a first down at the 25. Then came three brilliant completions to Berry, first a slant up the middle for 25 yards, followed by a diving reception at the 35 and finished by a quick hook at the 13. With 0:07 left, kicker Steve Myhra calmly entered the game and tied the score at 17.

Going into overtime, New York won the coin toss and elected to receive. After three plays, the Giants still needed a yard for a first down, so Don Chandler punted. The Colts took over on their 20, and Unitas started them down the field into history. To minimize the chances of a turnover, he kept the ball on the

ground. Dupre ran for 11 yards, then after two failed dives, Unitas gambled and shot a flare pass to Ameche in the flats, and The Horse bulled to another first down. Then, looking at third and long, Unitas executed what the analysts came to savor as the game's most crucial play. He dropped back to pass, hesitated, then broke to the left seemingly headed for the end, then stopped, faked a pass, then faded farther out. Berry, shaking and darting, broke open when Giant halfback Carl Karilivacz stumbled. Still, Unitas hesitated, motioning for Berry to go farther. Finally satisfied, he zipped the ball 21 yards to Berry's wide target, No. 82, for another first down at the New York 42. With the Giants plump for the fall, Unitas called the draw to Ameche. It went for 22 yards and another first down just inside the Giants 20. The New York defense tightened and stopped a run for a yard gain. But Unitas threw to Berry at the eight.

On the verge of football's great moment with nearly everyone in Yankee Stadium sensing an imminent field goal, a fan broke loose from the crowd and headed onto the field. Play was stopped for a full minute until police could entice him back into the stands. Unitas watched calmly, then crossed up the defense again when play resumed, throwing a sideline pass to tight end Jim Mutscheller, who went out of bounds at the one yard line. The next call was a dive to Ameche. The hole was wide, to say the least, and instead of defenders, The Horse was greeted by joyous Baltimore fans who rushed the end zone to greet him. Lost momentarily in the stupendous celebration were the statistics. Unitas had completed 26 of 40 passes for 349 yards. Berry

had caught 12 for 178 yards. The Giants, alas, had set a record with six fumbles.

The Giants and Colts returned to the title game the next year. Through three periods, their 1959 match-up seemed intent on bettering the 1958 contest. The Giants led 9-7 on three Pat Summerall field goals until the Colts erupted for three touchdowns in the fourth period to give Baltimore its second championship, 31-16. Unitas had done it again, completing 18 of 19 passes for 265 yards and two touchdowns.

He would take the Colts to the title game again in 1964 with a 12-2 record and what the oddsmakers thought was a clear advantage over the Cleveland Browns. Yet the Browns snared Unitas' passing game in a rapidly shifting defensive backfield and upset the Colts, 27-0.

Unitas also had a hand in Baltimore's 13-1 record in 1968, but he was injured during the season and played late and sparingly in the Super Bowl III debacle against Joe Namath and the New York Jets. He also was a factor in the Colts Super Bowl V championship. Yet he was an aging legend by then. His real brilliance came in 1958, when he gave football a performance for the ages.

Opposite bottom: *Colts quarterback Johnny Unitas releases a pass in a 36-14 win over Cleveland. He threw at least one touchdown in 47 straight games.*

Below: *Unitas, breaking loose from Carl Eller, threw four touchdown passes in this game versus Minnesota. He led the Colts to the NFL title in 1958 and 1959.*

Norm Van Brocklin

Norm Van Brocklin left his mark on pro football in many ways. He was the first quarterback to lead two different NFL teams to world championships. He has thrown for more yards in a single game (554) than any other pro quarterback. And he ranks among the best in passing statistics in the history of the sport.

But his major mark couldn't be measured, totalled or counted. For parts of three decades, his fiery competitiveness fuelled the Los Angeles Rams and the Philadelphia Eagles. He had a temper, and when he felt it was necessary, Van Brocklin wouldn't hesitate to fight, even if the opponent was a teammate in his own huddle.

Just out of the University of Oregon, Van Brocklin joined the Rams in 1949 and began sharing quarterbacking duties with veteran Bob Waterfield. The two of them drove the Rams to the 1949 title game, where they were shut out by the Philadelphia Eagles, 14-0. The next season, 1950, Van Brocklin led the league in passing, completing 127 of 233 attempts for 2061 yards and 18 touchdowns. Waterfield chipped in another 1600 yards or so passing to give Los Angeles the most potent offense in the business. In the championship game, they met the Cleveland Browns and led 28-20 in the fourth quarter before Otto Graham led the Browns to a great come-from-behind victory, 30-28.

The two teams returned to the finals the next year, and late in the game, Van Brocklin took over for Waterfield with the score tied at 17. With time running down, he zinged a 73-yard touchdown pass to his legendary receiver, Tom Fears, and the Rams claimed the title, 24-17. In 1952, Van Brocklin again led the league with 1736 yards passing. His 1954 season brought another passing crown. He completed 139 of 260 passes for 2637 yards and 13 touchdowns. Unfortunately, he also threw 21 interceptions.

In 1958, he was traded to the Philadelphia Eagles, where he and center linebacker Chuck Bednarik were the veteran stalwarts in a rebuilt team. They led the Eagles to a 10-2 record and the Eastern Conference crown in 1960. In the championship game, they faced Vince Lombardi's first great Green Bay Packer team. Van Brocklin passed for 204 yards and a touchdown in leading the Eagles to the 17-14 win. It was their first world championship since the 1940s. Van Brocklin retired after the season.

In 1971, he was inducted into the Hall of Fame. He died in 1983 at age 57.

Billy Wade

A prize for the Los Angeles Rams, Vanderbilt quarterback Billy Wade was the number one pick of the 1952 NFL draft. He made a few stops around the league before coming to the Chicago Bears in 1961. There he found his niche as a pro.

Wade started off right with the Bears by turning in an excellent 1961 season: 139 completions in 250 attempts for 2258 yards and 22 touchdowns against only 13 interceptions for a 93.7 passing rating. The Bears finished 8-6, a vast improvement over their 5-6-1 record of 1960. That record improved once again, in 1962, to 9-5.

But 1963 was the banner season in Wade's pro football career. Wade guided the Bears to the division title with an 11-1-2 record. Their opponents in the NFL championship game were the New York Giants with Y A Tittle. Wade showed his diversity, passing for 138 yards and rushing for another 34 and a touchdown, the winning score in the third quarter. The Bears won the world title, 14-10, providing a sense of accomplishment to Wade's career.

In six seasons with the Bears, he completed 767 of 1407 attempts (54.5 percent) for 9958 yards and 68 touchdowns.

Opposite: *Norm Van Brocklin of the Eagles hurls one in the 1961 Pro Bowl.*

Above: *Billy Wade, seen here in 1960 with the Rams, had his best years with the Bears.*

105

Left: *Bob Waterfield rolls for a big gain. He captured league passing crowns in 1946 and 1951.*
Above: *Waterfield entered the Hall of Fame in 1965.*

Bob Waterfield

Bob Waterfield entered the NFL in 1945 as a hotshot young quarterback, which, as things turned out, was just what the Cleveland Rams needed.

In his very first season, Waterfield led the franchise to the league's best record, 9-1, and the NFL's Western Division crown. In the process, he set a record for rookies, completing 171 passes for 1609 yards, an average completion of 9.409 yards. Sammy Baugh slightly bettered the yardage, with 1669, to win the league passing crown.

But the real passing challenge would be settled in the NFL championship game, where Waterfield's Rams met Baugh's Redskins. Baugh was ailing from a late-season rib injury and threw an incomplete pass that under the rules allowed Cleveland to score a safety. With the safety as padding, Waterfield threw two touchdown passes over the veteran Washington defense to lead the Rams to the championship, 15-14. Waterfield also was a fine placekicker and had kicked one of the extra points that helped Cleveland to victory.

For 1946, Waterfield won the league passing crown, completing 127 of 251 passes for 1747 yards and 18 touchdowns. But Chicago pushed the Rams, who had moved to Los Angeles, out of the championship picture. Waterfield wouldn't take his team back to the title game until 1949, when he teamed with rookie quarterback Norm Van Brocklin (in those days one-platoon

football teams regularly used two or more quarterbacks). Together, they led the Rams to an 8-2-2 record and the National crown. Their receivers were Tom Fears, Elroy 'Crazy Legs' Hirsch, Dick Hoerner and Bob Shaw. Their grand air game was grounded by the LA rainy season and the Philadelphia Eagles' defense, as the Rams lost the title game, 14-0.

For 1950, Van Brocklin and Waterfield teamed up again to drive the Rams to the title game, this time against the Cleveland Browns. Van Brocklin had led the league in passing, but Waterfield opened the championship game with an 82-yard touchdown pass to Glenn Davis on the first play. The contest was nip-and-tuck after that, but late in the game, Waterfield had driven the Rams to a 28-20 lead. From there, the Browns put on two drives to win, 30-28, in one of the greatest comebacks in the history of the league.

The next year, 1951, Waterfield found some retribution, as well as another league passing crown and NFL title for his team. On the season, he completed 88 of 176 passes for 1566 yards and 13 touchdowns. With an 8-4 record, the Rams took the National crown, then zipped the Browns, 24-17, for the NFL title. Waterfield contributed three extra points and a 17-yard field goal to the scoring.

He retired from his playing career after the 1952 season and was elected to the Hall of Fame in 1965. Waterfield died in 1983 at age 62.

Danny White

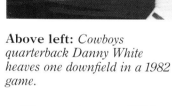

Above left: *Cowboys quarterback Danny White heaves one downfield in a 1982 game.*

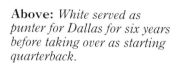

Above: *White served as punter for Dallas for six years before taking over as starting quarterback.*

A record-setting passer at Arizona State, Danny White was selected in the third round of the 1974 draft by the Dallas Cowboys. For six years he did the team's punting chores and served as understudy to Roger Staubach. In 1980, after Staubach retired, White became the Cowboys' starting quarterback and faced the challenge of replacing a legend.

His first two seasons out of the gate, 1980-81, White passed for more than 3000 yards each. He repeated that feat again in 1983 and 1985. For the 1981 season, he finished second in the NFC passing race, throwing for 3098 yards and 22 touchdowns.

Those statistics, however, meant little to Dallas fans who were used to Staubach's runs at the Super Bowl. In 1980, White led the Cowboys to a wild card spot with a 12-4 record. In the playoffs they eliminated Los Angeles, 34-13, as White passed for 190 yards and three touchdowns. The next week against Atlanta, he threw for 322 yards and three touchdown passes, including two in the fourth quarter, to lead the Cowboys in one of the great comebacks in playoff history, a 30-27 win. The NFC championship game, however, was a different story, as the Philadelphia Eagles dominated, 20-7.

The next year, White took Dallas to the Eastern Division title with a 12-4 record and blasted Tampa Bay in the playoffs, 28-0, but then lost to Joe Montana and the San Francisco 49ers on Montana's classic late-game touchdown pass to Dwight Clark. The play overshadowed White's comeback effort that drove Dallas to 10 points in the fourth quarter. Down 21-17, the Cowboys had just taken a 27-21 lead when the 49ers struck.

In the strike-shortened 1982 season, White took Dallas to the NFC championship game for a third straight year, only to lose a third time, 31-17, to the Washington Redskins. Under his guidance, Dallas teams won a playoff spot in 1983 and the division crown in 1985, but failed to advance to the NFC title game both times. White was off to one of his best seasons in 1986, when injuries knocked him out of competition.

White set club records for season yardage (3980) and touchdown passes (29) in 1983. That year he recorded the third highest single-game completion percentage in the history of the league, hitting 21 of 24 passes against Philadelphia for 87.50 percent.

White's career passing statistics rank him among the 20 highest rated quarterbacks in league history.

Doug Williams

The Tampa Bay Buccaneers selected Grambling quarterback Doug Williams in the first round of the 1978 draft, and he paid almost immediate dividends for the young franchise, taking them to the playoffs three times in five years.

In 1979, Williams led Tampa Bay to the NFC Central Division title with a 10-6 record. In the playoffs, Williams gave the team the first postseason victory in its history, a 24-17 win over the Philadelphia Eagles.

In 1981, Williams again took the Bucs to the divisional title and the playoffs by throwing for 3563 yards, a club record. In the playoffs, the protection from Williams' offensive line broke down in the face of the Dallas Cowboys' pass rush. He was sacked four times and forced into throwing four interceptions as Dallas won, 38-0. Tampa Bay gained the playoffs again in the strike-shortened 1982 season as Williams pushed the team into the Super Bowl tournament with a 5-4 record. There, they again lost to Dallas, 30-17, in the first round.

After a stint in the USFL, Williams signed with the Washington Redskins as a backup quarterback to Jay Schroeder, and was starting quarterback at Super Bowl XXII versus the Denver Broncos. The first black quarterback in Super Bowl history, Williams led a 42-10 pasting of the Broncos which featured an amazing second-quarter comeback from a 10-0 deficit: for the quarter, Williams completed 9 of 11 attempts for 228 yards and four touchdowns. The Redskins had scored a record 35 points while possessing the ball for only 5:54 of the quarter. A second-half touchdown run by Redskins rookie running back Timmy Smith closed out the scoring. MVP Williams' 340 yards passing was a new Super Bowl record, as was the Redskins' 602 yards total offense. Doug Williams had finally proven his mettle to the football world.

Jim Zorn

The Seattle Seahawks opened their franchise in 1976, and after some indecision, the management settled on free-agent rookie quarterback Jim Zorn as the team's regular. Zorn responded by setting a passing yardage record for a rookie, 2571 yards. He also set NFL rookie records for passes attempted (439) and completed (208). Over the next nine seasons, he would set club records for passing yardage (20,042) and touchdown passes (107).

By his and the franchise's third year, Zorn had led the Seahawks from the cellar to a winning record, 9-7, good enough to tie for second in the AFC Western Division. They also finished 9-7 in 1979, but skidded into losing after that.

After serving as a backup to Dave Krieg for a time, Zorn left Seattle after the 1984 season and joined the Green Bay Packers, where he shared playing time with several quarterbacks. After a stint in the Canadian Football League, he retired from playing in 1986.

Opposite: *Big Doug Williams of Tampa Bay set a club record in 1981 with 3563 passing yards.*

Below: *Jim Zorn calls out his signals behind his Seahawk line. He was Seattle's first quarterback, playing from 1976 to 1984.*

THE 100 GREATEST QUARTERBACKS

BY RANK

1. Johnny Unitas
2. Otto Graham
3. Dan Marino
4. Roger Staubach
5. Joe Montana
6. Bart Starr
7. YA Tittle
8. Norm Van Brocklin
9. Terry Bradshaw
10. Dan Fouts
11. Sid Luckman
12. Sammy Baugh
13. Bobby Layne
14. Fran Tarkenton
15. Len Dawson
16. Sonny Jurgensen
17. Dutch Clark
18. Jim Plunkett
19. Ken Stabler
20. Bob Griese
21. Joe Namath
22. George Blanda
23. Bob Waterfield
24. Ken Anderson
25. Arnie Herber
26. Roman Gabriel
27. Tommy Thompson
28. Joe Theismann
29. Bert Jones
30. Phil Simms
31. Ron Jaworski
32. Paddy Driscoll
33. John Brodie
34. Don Meredith

35. Jimmy Conzelman
36. Jim McMahon
37. Charlie Conerly
38. Ed Danowski
39. Daryle Lamonica
40. Doug Williams
41. Norm Snead
42. Jack Kemp
43. Frank Ryan
44. Milt Plum
45. Craig Morton
46. Jim Hart
47. Charley Johnson
48. Ace Parker
49. Earl Morrall
50. Archie Manning
51. Cecil Isbell
52. Tobin Rote
53. Brian Sipe
54. Danny White
55. John Elway
56. Johnny Lujack
57. John Hadl
58. Lynn Dickey
59. Babe Parilli
60. Billy Kilmer
61. Billy Wade
62. Joe Ferguson
63. Paul Christman
64. Frank Tripucka
65. Steve Grogan
66. Neil Lomax
67. Joe Kapp
68. Ed Brown

69. Dave Krieg
70. Tony Eason
71. Ken O'Brien
72. Jim Kelly
73. Tommy O'Connell
74. Bernie Kosar
75. Eddie LeBaron
76. Harry Newman
77. Parker Hall
78. Dan Pastorini
79. Warren Moon
80. Gary Danielson
81. James Harris
82. Vince Ferragamo
83. Frank Filchock
84. Boomer Esiason
85. Tom Flores
86. Bill Kenney
87. Steve Bartkowski
88. Tommy Kramer
89. Jay Schroeder
90. Richard Todd
91. Zeke Bratkowski
92. Bernie Masterson
93. Pete Beathard
94. Pat Haden
95. Rudy Bukich
96. Greg Cook
97. Greg Landry
98. Steve DeBerg
99. Bobby Douglass
100. Jim Zorn

Opposite: *Johnny Unitas completed 2830 out of 5186 passes in his 18-year career, throwing 290 TDs for 40,239 yards. Yet his classic style, audacious play, and brilliant leadership is what really ranks him as one of the very best to ever line up behind center.*

INDEX

Acknowledgments

The author and publisher would like to thank the following people who helped with the preparation of this book: Jean Chiaramonte Martin, who edited it; Mike Rose, who designed it; Lynn Leedy, who did the picture research; and Cynthia Klein, who prepared the index.

Photo Credits

The Bettmann Archive Inc: 16 (top), 64 (top).
The Chicago Bears: 60.
Focus on Sports: 2-3, 5, 6 (both), 7 (both), 11 (both), 13, 18 (bottom), 21, 22 (both), 23, 24 (top), 25 (both), 26 (both), 27, 28 (both), 29, 31 (both), 34 (both), 35, 38, 39 (all 4), 42, 43, 46 (top & bottom right), 47, 48, 51, 52 (both), 53, 56, 57 (both), 68 (both), 70 (both), 72 (both), 73, 75, 77, 78 (bottom), 79 (top), 84 (both), 87, 88 (both), 91 (bottom), 92 (right), 93, 95 (both), 96 (both), 107 (both), 108, 109.
Pro Football Hall of Fame: 8, 9 (top), 17 (top), 24 (bottom), 30, 36 (bottom), 44, 49 (both), 61 (all 3), 65 (top), 76, 83 (bottom), 85 (right), 92 (left), 94, 99 (left), 104, 106 (both).
UPI/Bettmann Newsphotos: 1, 9 (bottom), 10 (both), 12 (both), 14, 15 (both), 16 (bottom), 17 (bottom), 18 (top), 19 (both), 20-1, 32, 33, 36 (top), 37, 40-1, 41, 45 (both), 46 (left), 50 (both), 54 (both), 55, 58-9, 59, 62, 63, 64 (bottom), 65 (bottom), 66-7, 67, 69, 71, 74, 78 (top), 79 (bottom), 80, 81 (both), 82, 83 (top), 85 (left), 86 (both), 89, 90, 91 (top), 97, 98, 99 (right), 100 (both), 101, 102, 103, 105, 110.